Scents and Flavors

Letter from the General Editor

The Library of Arabic Literature makes available Arabic editions and English translations of significant works of Arabic literature, with an emphasis on the seventh to nineteenth centuries. The Library of Arabic Literature thus includes texts from the pre-Islamic era to the cusp of the modern period, and encompasses a wide range of genres, including poetry, poetics, fiction, religion, philosophy, law, science, travel writing, history, and historiography.

Books in the series are edited and translated by internationally recognized scholars. They are published in parallel-text and English-only editions in both print and electronic formats. PDFs of Arabic editions are available for free download. The Library of Arabic Literature also publishes distinct scholarly editions with critical apparatus and a separate Arabic-only series aimed at young readers.

The Library encourages scholars to produce authoritative Arabic editions, accompanied by modern, lucid English translations, with the ultimate goal of introducing Arabic's rich literary heritage to a general audience of readers as well as to scholars and students.

The Library of Arabic Literature is supported by a grant from the New York University Abu Dhabi Institute and is published by NYU Press.

Philip F. Kennedy
General Editor, Library of Arabic Literature

About this Paperback

This paperback edition differs in a few respects from its dual-language hardcover predecessor. Because of the compact trim size the pagination has changed. Material that referred to the Arabic edition has been updated to reflect the English-only format, and other material has been corrected and updated where appropriate. For information about the Arabic edition on which this English translation is based and about how the LAL Arabic text was established, readers are referred to the hardcover.

Scents and Flavors

A Syrian Cookbook

TRANSLATED BY
Charles Perry

FOREWORD BY
Claudia Roden

VOLUME EDITORS
Michael Cooperson
Shawkat M. Toorawa

NEW YORK UNIVERSITY PRESS
New York

NEW YORK UNIVERSITY PRESS
New York

Library of Congress Cataloging-in-Publication Data
Names: Perry, Charles, 1941– translator. | Roden, Claudia, other.
Title: Scents and flavors : a Syrian cookbook / translated by Charles Perry ; foreword by Claudia Roden ; volume editors, Michael Cooperson, Shawkat M. Toorawa.
Other titles: Kitab al-wusla ila al-habib. English.
Description: New York : New York University Press, [2020] | Series: Library of Arabic literature | Previously published: 2017. | Includes bibliographical references and index. | Arabic and English. | Summary: "This popular thirteenth-century Syrian cookbook is an ode to what its anonymous author calls the 'greater part of the pleasure of this life,' namely the consumption of food and drink, as well as the fragrances that garnish the meals and the diners who enjoy them. Organized like a meal, Scents and Flavors opens with appetizers and juices and proceeds through main courses, side dishes, and desserts."— Provided by publisher.
Identifiers: LCCN 2019049983 (print) | LCCN 2019049984 (ebook) | ISBN 9781479800810 (paperback) | ISBN 9781479800827 (ebook) | ISBN 9781479800834 (ebook)
Subjects: LCSH: Cooking, Syrian. | LCGFT: Cookbooks.
Classification: LCC TX725.S9 S33413 2020 (print) | LCC TX725.S9 (ebook) | DDC 641.595691—dc23
LC record available at https://lccn.loc.gov/2019049983
LC ebook record available at https://lccn.loc.gov/2019049984

Series design and composition by Nicole Hayward
Typeset in Adobe Text
Manufactured in the United States of America

10 9 8 7 6 5 4 3 2 1

Contents

Foreword

CLAUDIA RODEN

Sixty years ago I was enthralled when I came across an essay on this medieval Syrian cookbook at the British Library in London. It was a sociological study by the French Orientalist Maxime Rodinson entitled *Récherches sur les manuscrits Arabes relatifs à la cuisine.* Rodinson listed names of the dishes in the book and gave an indication of what they were, but he only translated nine of its roughly 690 recipes. Many of the names—*sanbūsak, kaʿk, mulūkhiyyah, kunāfah,* to give a few—were of recipes I had been collecting from relatives whose roots were in the Jewish community of Aleppo. It was thrilling to know that our foods had a history. It confirmed our ancestry.

Three of my grandparents had come to Egypt as part of a huge emigration at the end of the 19th century when the Suez Canal was built and Aleppo lost its prime position on the trade routes from the East. They settled in a newly developed quarter of Cairo called Sakakini that became almost exclusively Syrian. My father said that you knew by the smells wafting in the street and by the sound of the pounding of mortars what people were cooking. But there had been no cookbooks in Egypt. Recipes had been handed down in families. And now the living link was endangered since my family, along with other Jews, many of whom originated in different parts of the old Ottoman lands, had left Egypt in a hurry *en masse* after the 1956 Suez War.

Ever since that day in the British Library I had longed for a translation of that book. Charles Perry's *Scents and Flavors* is the first. It is an extraordinary, monumental, meticulous work of enormous erudition and dedication, a real labor of love, by a man who also knows how to cook.

Recipe writing was an Arab tradition that started in Baghdad in the 10th century, when cooking was transformed into an art that reached magnificent heights. The banquets at the royal courts were proverbial for their variety and lavishness. The search for the most delicious combinations of food was the preoccupation of a distinguished society of gourmets. The caliphs commissioned people to invent dishes, to write poems about food and to sing their praise at gatherings. Poets, astrologers, astronomers, scholars, princes, and even caliphs took pleasure in writing about food. And doctors wrote medical books that included chapters on dietetics and gave recipes.

By the 13th century, collections of recipes were being commissioned and compiled by scribes, and these were recopied incorporating earlier collections and new additions.

The codifying of recipes would have started in the huge court kitchens that were staffed by a large number of cooks, where cooking had to be recorded so that it could be easily passed on and the instructions read out to illiterate cooks. It is through these books that recipes filtered down to aspiring middle classes. Of the five major volumes of the time, each of which had six to seven hundred recipes, *Scents and Flavors* was the most popular, a bestseller. It is likely to have had more than one author, but it is uniformly organized with chapters and sub chapters, and numerous variations to recipes, and the same spirit of conviviality and joyful appreciation of food runs through it.

The book represents the cooking in the kitchens of the Ayyubid court and of the Syrian nobility. It features recipes from different parts of the Muslim Empire—they are Persian, Baghdadi, Turkish, Egyptian, Moroccan, Bedouin, Georgian. It was the period of the

Crusades and the European influence can be seen in the "Frankish" dishes.

It describes the cuisine of a sensual society, very rich in flavors and aromas. The first chapter is of incense and perfumes for use on the body before a banquet and the last is about flower-scented waters for washing hands after the meal. A huge number of spices and aromatics are used in a variety of combinations and together with herbs. Syria had an important role in the camel caravan trade from the East and Aleppo was famously a station on the spice route and its spice bazaar was the beating heart of the city.

Visual appeal is given importance. Saffron and turmeric are used for color; chopped almonds, rose petals, and pomegranate seeds as garnish. As expected of a princely cuisine, expensive ingredients such as chicken and lamb are much used, but so are vegetables, pulses, grain, and fruit.

Techniques are elaborate and sophisticated. Vegetables are hollowed out and stuffed, elegant little parcels are made with wrappings of pastry. Vegetables are preserved with salt and vinegar, lemon juice, and mustard. Fruit are cooked in syrup and crystallized. There is smoke-drying. Meat is preserved in its own fat. Sauces are thickened with bread and with ground almonds or ground rice.

The mysterious author, or main author, does not reveal his name. But he has a very personal voice. He tells you when a dish is delicious and really worth making and when a recipe is not the best version but that he included it because he had to, for the sake of completeness and in case you might like it. He also has views on health and medicine.

We learn about so much more than food. We learn about protocol, manners, and customs; about the spread of agricultural crops in the Empire and the large-scale transport of foodstuffs from one part to another; of the importance of religion. God and the prophet are invoked, Qur'anic prohibitions and regulations are observed, and no pork or wine is used.

The publication of this book will be an important resource to anyone interested in the history of the Middle East and the Middle Ages, to sociologists and anthropologists, and to anyone interested in food. Food writers and cooks could find it fascinating and might be inspired to do their own take on some of the dishes.

With the huge popularity of Middle Eastern food today, much of what is featured in Charles Perry's *Scents and Flavors* will be familiar. You might recognize the lamb with apricots or sour cherries, the stuffed eggplants with spiced minced meat, the pastries stuffed with chopped almonds sugar and rose water, or the milk pudding with ground rice garnished with pistachios and pomegranate seeds. And you will be able to find almost all the ingredients—couscous, chickpeas, yogurt, tahini, pomegranate syrup, sumac, poppy and sesame seeds, fenugreek, dried rose petals, and rose buds.

There is something fascinating and moving about historical recipes. They are an intimate link with the past, revealing the sensuous quality, the tastes and smells and feel of worlds gone by, and they also tell us a great deal about the past.

Claudia Roden
London

Acknowledgments

The author earnestly thanks his editor, Michael Cooperson, and his outside reader, David Waines. Their readiness to engage the issues of these ancient recipes was a delight.

He also wishes to thank the librarians who made manuscripts available to a scholar who had no academic affiliation—clearly an unfamiliar situation to some of them—and in particular the librarian of the Waqfiyyah Library in 1980, who seemed the embodiment of the love of learning. Wearing a white scholar's robe and speaking beautiful formal Arabic, he glowed with delight as he discussed the manuscript treasures of his little room, oblivious to the fact that Aleppo was under martial law and encircled by tanks.

Introduction

Cookbooks are commonplace today, but they are a late development in world literature. In antiquity we find only three Babylonian clay tablets and a single Roman cookbook compiled in the second century; after that, nothing more for the next 800 years. Then there was a sudden explosion of cookbooks in Arabic. From the tenth through the thirteenth centuries, Arabic speakers were, so far as we know, the only people in the world who were writing cookbooks.

They had elaborated the idea from the personal recipe collections that had been fashionable for gentlemen of the pre-Islamic Persian court to keep. The Abbasid caliphs adopted this along with many other Persian practices, such as cooking contests among the ruler's boon companions. In the tenth century, a scribe named Abū Muḥammad al-Muẓaffar ibn Naṣr ibn Sayyār compiled a large collection of Baghdad court recipes for an unnamed patron who wanted to know what "kings and caliphs and lords and leaders" ate—this probably established the idea of the cookbook for the Arab reading public. To judge from the fact that most surviving manuscripts show evidence of dozens of generations of copying, cookbooks formed a regular part of a commercial scribe's business.

These books were intended for practical household use and more or less cheaply copied (in fact, it is a bit surprising that so many have survived to our day). Moreover, it is clear that scribes were uniformly ignorant of cooking. As a result, cookery manuscripts tend to be marred by a remarkable number of errors. We can be grateful for one thing—only one of them, the Cairo manuscript Lām 5076, shows the wear and staining that indicates that it was actually handled in the kitchen. The fact that recipes vacillate between second-person instructions and third-person descriptions of the cooking process suggests that recipes were typically read out to the cook and the book was then replaced in the household library.

The golden age of cookbooks was the thirteenth century, which produced five major volumes of several hundred recipes each, two of them from Spain and North Africa and the rest from the eastern Arab world, as well as several smaller collections. *Scents and Flavors the Banqueter Favors* (*Kitāb al-Wuṣlah ilā l-Ḥabīb fī Waṣf al-Ṭayyibāt wal-Ṭīb*) contains 635 recipes (nearly 700 in some versions of the text) and was the bestseller of the age, to judge from the fact that more copies of it have survived than of all the other medieval cookbooks combined. It primarily represents the cuisine of the Ayyubid rulers of thirteenth-century Syria—the author often mentions visiting various Ayyubid noble households.

One reason for its popularity was its systematic organization. In most chapters the recipes are carefully numbered and variations are numbered as sub-recipes. The clarity is a little spoiled by the fact that a few recipes disappeared during the long generations of copying and many more were added without being numbered. This is very noticeable in Chapter 7, which scrupulously announces that the following fifty-five recipes "do not belong to the book." Nevertheless, readers doubtless appreciated the sense that they had before them a well-organized volume.

Another reason for the book's popularity can be seen from its title, literally "the link to the friend, concerning good things to eat and perfumes." Medieval Arab cuisine was highly scented, not only with herbs, nuts, and spices but sometimes also ingredients we would consider to be perfumes, such as rose water, musk or ambergris, occasionally even incense. (That tradition is not entirely dead: in modern Syria the pudding *nishawayyeh* may still be perfumed with sandalwood.)

The medieval banquet was a feast for the nose, and the diners were expected to make their own contribution. Before the meal, they would have bathed at the hammam and then perfumed themselves. There were specific perfumes for the hands, the face, the hair and even clothing, which was often aromatized by holding it over burning incense. One recipe in the book refers to a pocket incense burner made of filigreed silver which could scent one's clothes continuously. As a result, medieval Arab readers were not surprised to find recipes for perfumes and even breath fresheners and antiperspirants in cookbooks.

A handful of recipes (for perfumes as well as foods) reference medieval medical ideas, such as the need to balance the humors or to match foods to the humoral nature of an individual. Another individual matter was how much store a given diner actually set by medical theory. Doctors may have warned that eggplant caused cancer and madness, but the poet Kushājim, for one, defiantly said, "The doctor makes ignorant fun of me for loving eggplant, but I will not give it up."

No book addressed the subject in as much detail as *Scents and Flavors*, which is organized roughly in parallel with the stages of a banquet. The first chapter is on incense and perfumes. Following a few short chapters on beverages and miscellaneous necessities come the chapters on main dishes, followed by chapters on pickles, snacks and sweets, which did not have regular place in the banquet, then a chapter on perfumed preparations for cleaning the hands after eating. The final chapter is on the fragrant distilled waters which diners would splash on themselves at the end of the banquet.

Characteristics of the Cuisine

We may not expect to perfume ourselves so extravagantly at dinner, but reading about it gives a glimpse of the seductive splendor of a medieval banquet. The cuisine of this book is definitely banquet food, special-occasion food. Not only is it highly aromatic, it is thoroughly luxurious. Many simple stews are enriched with meatballs and garnished with pastries and tidbits of various kinds.

Since diners ate with their hands, many recipes concern themselves with achieving a suitable consistency. Dishes may be thickened by cooking them down or by adding a thickener such as ground nuts. Some foods were thickened to a suitable texture for picking up with a piece of bread, like modern-day Syrian snacks such as hummus with tahini. The book also refers to eating certain dishes with a utensil unattested elsewhere, a *jamjā'*, which must have resembled a soup spoon.

In our time, meat is aged for days, even weeks, by being hung in a cold locker or refrigerated in vacuum-pack in order to give the enzymes in the meat time to tenderize it. In the cuisine of this book, however, meat is cooked the day it is butchered, which means it is relatively tough. When a recipe describes the frying of meat, therefore, there is usually an additional step of boiling it, either before or after, to achieve the desired tenderness. This is also true of chicken. One recipe instructs cooks to tire chickens out by chasing them about before killing them, a practice inherited from the Persians. This may strike a modern cook as totally wrong, since we now know that when an animal is killed without stress, its cells continue to use up their fuel and since fresh oxygen is no longer available, the lactic acid produced by this process can't be broken down and serves to tenderize the meat. But as the food science writer Harold McGee points out, stressing the chickens might have a point: it speeds the onset of rigor mortis, which occurs when muscles run out of fuel and the contractile proteins lock into place, and thus also speeds the passing of the rigor.

Some now forgotten foods were created by microbial action. One is *murrī*, a salty liquid with a flavor closely resembling soy sauce which was produced by mold-culturing barley and adding spices such as fennel. It was very popular in Spain and Iraq but makes only a single appearance (§6.47) in this book, which gives no recipe for it. *Kāmakh baghdādī* (§8.66) was a semi-liquid cheese made by aging milk with yogurt and salt, which preserve it from spoilage while the microbes that produce the familiar cheese flavor do their work. One recipe for pickled capers minutely describes the process of making a semi-liquid blue cheese. Certain sorts of cheese were added to dishes as they cook, a practice that has disappeared from Arab cuisine.

The recipes reflect the culinary situation of the landlocked corridor that extends from Aleppo to Damascus. Fresh fish are completely absent and even salt fish play only a small part; there is even a condiment that counterfeits dried fish with walnuts and sesame. To give dishes a sour flavor, recipes may call for citrus fruits imported from the coast but, as in the cuisine of Aleppo today, very often local sour ingredients such as pomegranate or sumac berry are preferred. Somewhat less use is made of lamb fat and sesame oil for frying than in Iraqi cookbooks and greater use is made of olive oil, though it often appears as a flavoring rather than a frying medium. And sesame oil is sometimes toasted, as it commonly is in China, for use as a flavoring.

For baking, the recipes call for the clay oven that predominates in Iraq and points farther east and also the Roman-style brick oven widespread in Spain and North Africa. Together with the heritage of the Perso-Arab cuisine of the ninth-century Baghdad court, *Scents and Flavors* shows the beginnings of Turkish influence on Syria's repertoire of breads and pastas, including one interesting pastry with a Turkish name, *qarni yārūq*, which resembles a deconstructed baklava or, more exactly, a baklava *avant la lettre,* since the first baklava recipes would not be recorded until the sixteenth century. Included also are some preparations learned from the Byzantines and the Crusaders, who still held territory in the region.

Among the many herbs and spices called for were some that play little part in Arab cuisine today, such as caraway and the bitter herb rue. Soap was mostly perfumed with spices and rose water, any of which might also appear in the dishes that followed—one reason for washing before the meal might have been to remove any perfume on the hand that might conflict with the flavors of the food. The preparations for washing after the meal are based on washing soda (sodium carbonate, still a common ingredient in laundry powders), which would very effectively remove any fat or oil on the hands by the chemical reaction of saponification, which in effect converted fat into soap. They always included a neutral extender such as rice flour because washing soda is harsh on the skin.

Sugar had first been refined from cane sap in India, but it was in the Arab world—presumably Baghdad, to begin with—that confectioners began to study the higher densities of sugar syrup which are the foundation of modern candies and sweets. In the eighteenth century, European confectioners developed a standard for minutely distinguishing the stages, based largely on observing the behavior of a drop of syrup in cold water, whether it formed a thread or a soft ball or a firmer texture. These are described in every substantial cookbook, such as Auguste Escoffier's *Guide Culinaire*. The pioneering Arab confectioners used a mixture of criteria: subjective observations like "thin," "thick," "sticky," and "of a proper texture"; whether the syrup would form brittle threads between the fingers or drip in a continuous thread or in a broad sheet; and its behavior when placed in the mouth, such as chewiness. The recipes here clearly distinguish at least eight densities of sugar syrup, not counting hard candy, which is not often thought of as syrup.

The most esteemed dish of the age was *jūdhāb* (or *jūdhābah*). This was a sweet, generally of a pudding consistency,[1] sandwiched between two layers of thin flatbread and placed in a baking dish. A chicken was hung in the chimney of a clay oven to roast in the high heat. When it was nearly done, the *jūdhāb* would be inserted in the oven to catch the fat and meat juices as they dripped. Finally, both chicken and *jūdhāb* would be removed, the chicken would be chopped up, and the diner would receive a slice of *jūdhāb* festively topped with meat. This was such a familiar preparation that recipes sometimes omit steps such as sandwiching between the flatbreads, roasting the chicken, or even sending the *jūdhāb* to the oven. The dishes *khabīṣ al-lawz* and *samīdhiyyah* are written in a way that suggests that they were *jūdhāb*s, or at least could be treated as such. Such was the popularity of the dish that several recipes in the chicken chapter (§§5.2, 5.16, and 5.26) are, in effect, *jūdhāb*s that don't require a clay oven.

Some less familiar starch foods appear in this book, alongside the well-known pilaf (*aruzz mufalfal*) and couscous (*kuskusū*). *Tabbālah* was a concoction of rice, noodles, and meat which was often garnished with other meat products. *Ṭuṭmāj*, the traditional pasta of the Turkish nomads, was cut into squares, rather than into thin strips like the Persian *rishtā*. Its shape explains why recipes often say to roll out *ṭuṭmāj* when producing a sheet of dough to be stuffed.

The Chapters

Like other medieval Arab cookbooks, *Scents and Flavors* begins with an introduction that cites the Qur'an to show that enjoyment of food is no sin. Its author claims to have tested every one of the recipes that follow. Whether or not this is true, in many cases he does clearly speak from experience (and decided opinion).

In the first chapter, on perfume, the favored aromatics are often expensive ones: ambergris, musk, and agarwood, an incense resembling sandalwood but sweeter and richer. Rose water and pungent camphor were also common (not only in perfumes but in both sweet and savory dishes). Aromatic resins such as labdanum and costus frequently enter into compound perfumes.

Perfume ingredients could be kneaded into convenient shapes and enjoyed in that form, but could also be lit like incense—the distinction between perfume and incense was by no means absolute, and incense was the favorite way to scent clothing. There were liquid perfumes based on oils, particularly the mild, fragrant ben oil (*duhn al-bān*), the basis of the men's hand perfume *ghāliyah*, but alcohol-based perfumes were unknown. There were also fragrant powders (*dharīrah*), which often had lighter floral fragrances. Some of these perfumes were considered to have medicinal properties.

The beverages in Chapter 2 include peculiar-sounding preparations that resemble starchy soups which have been allowed to ferment. Doubtless they were not fermented enough to intoxicate, though a honey-based drink called *ṣurmār* suggests that adding hops could give it intoxicating properties, a practice of the Kipchak Turkic nations. Some may have resembled the Turkish soured grain drink *boza*, but flavored with fruit juice and spices. Other beverages in this chapter are based on fruits, but with unusual additives such as incense or medicinal ingredients.

Chapter 3 describes sour fruit juices, some for drinking but mostly treated to be preserved for use in the kitchen out of season.

Chapter 4 is devoted to the proper method of rendering the tasty fat of the Middle Eastern fat-tailed sheep and, perhaps somewhat surprisingly, how to color it red, yellow, or green.

Chapter 5 is wholly devoted to chicken, which is not surprising since chicken was a luxury food before the development of mechanized plucking. The chapter opens with sections on roast chicken, and chicken with spiced stuffing, put on or in the chicken *after* it was cooked. Galantine, chicken skin stuffed with meat and then reassembled to resemble a whole chicken, was probably a novelty dish to amuse guests. Among the wide miscellany that follows are sections on chicken cooked with various fruits such as apples, quinces, or mulberries, or cooked with nuts—walnuts, pistachios, hazelnuts, and the like—called *ḥalāwat al-dajāj* or "chicken sweetmeats," perhaps so styled because medieval sweetmeats were regularly flavored with nuts.

The longest chapter by far is Chapter 6, which accounts for about a quarter of the book. It is all about lamb, cooked in a variety of ways, including roasting in the oven, frying, braising, and baking on bread in pizza fashion. A whole lamb spitted over two fires is said to be a recipe learned from Europeans, and lamb baked in an earth pit is a Bedouin dish. There are numerous stews with vegetables; the fruits that figure are less acid ones than in chicken recipes: quince, apple, apricot, and banana. Meat also appears in starch dishes: pilaf, couscous, noodles, and *harīsah*, a sort of porridge of crushed wheat. As in the chicken chapter, the lamb dishes are also flavored with sour ingredients such as vinegar, sumac, and lemon juice. Specific meat recipes include *narjisiyyah*, which was topped with poached eggs, producing a fanciful resemblance to the flower poet's narcissus, and *dīnāriyyah*, in which sliced carrots suggested the gold coin dinar. The similarity was greater than today because carrots then were yellow, rather than orange.

Chapter 7 covers sweets, including multiple recipes for crepes, rice pudding and pistachio pudding (both kinds of pudding could contain chicken breast, like the medieval European *blanc manger* and the present-day Turkish *tavuk göğsü*) and dishes resembling noodle puddings made by cutting a very thin flatbread into strips. (In all but one manuscript of *Scents and Flavors*, these recipes are followed by a larger collection of recipes that had probably circulated on their own at one time, since most also appear in other thirteenth-century cookbooks.)

Following the sweets comes a section on baked goods. It is relatively short, presumably because breads were readily available from bakers; this doubtless also explains why the recipes are for unusual breads. Among the several recipes for *kaʿk*, usually a sort of *biscotti* which is cooked twice for crispness, is a startling one that includes a technique of boiling bread before baking it—the basis of making pretzels and bagels. The result even looked like a bagel, because *kaʿk* was ring-shaped. Another type of bread is kneaded with pieces of cheese. Two flatbreads, said to be European and Armenian, have a spiced topping of eggs. Several puddings have been shoehorned into the end of this section, though logically they should have appeared among the sweets.

Chapter 8 covers pickles, most of them soured with vinegar, yogurt, or sour fruit juice; and one recipe uses sourdough, a technique still known in northern Iraq. Olives, raisins, capers, salt fish, and salted lemons do not need to be preserved, so the recipes given are not, properly speaking, for pickles but for condiments made from those ingredients. The pickles section ends with a category of sauces or condiments called *ṣalṣ*, which automatically suggests the European word *salsa* and the idea that they were learned from the Crusaders. Only the first of them actually resembles a medieval European sauce. The rest are clearly Middle Eastern, mostly consisting of ground nuts mixed with flavorings and a sour ingredient. In another thirteenth-century book, *Kitāb Waṣf al-Aṭʿimah al-Muʿtādah*, *ṣalṣ* was associated with fresh fish.

The chapter on pickles ends with a number of recipes for *bawārid*, literally "cold dishes." Most are cooked vegetable preparations, but they include egg dishes and the savory pastry *sanbūsak*. These were all snacks eaten outside the context of a meal, much like today's mezze. Connoisseurs had a charming custom of sending each other baskets of these little treats, sometimes accompanied by a dedicatory poem.[2]

Diners ate with their hands, so great attention was paid to cleanliness, the subject of Chapter 9. After the meal, diners washed their hands with powders based on washing soda obtained from the ashes of a sort of tumbleweed known as *ushnān*, which gave its name to this category. Before eating, they would have washed with perfumed soap, so a soap recipe appears here but the focus is on *ushnān*, possibly because the aromatic possibilities of soap are limited, while the host could make a wide variety of highly scented powders, from heavy and musky to spicy or floral. The *ushnān* recipes are quoted from various books on perfumery (most of which have not survived), and consequently they are written in more formal Arabic than the other recipes in the book.

Chapter 10 gives recipes for a number of fragrant waters (types of rose water in particular) including ones tinted in ways guaranteed not to stain diners' clothes. Other waters are distilled from herbs, spices, and perfume and incense ingredients. The two most interesting ingredients are palm spathe, the bract that surrounds immature palm flowers—it is said to have a scent resembling vanilla—and the combination of cucumber and basil, which was apparently a common rubdown after a steam bath.

History of the Book

Rare is the cookbook at any time that has even claimed to be the sole product of its author. The writer of a cookbook is more exactly a compiler. He may invent the occasional dish or striking variation, but recipes by nature are the shared property of their time and place. Cookbook writers may credit the source of a recipe, particularly when it is one to boast of, such as an aristocratic household, but usually the recipe is just whichever version of the dish the writer has encountered and liked best. More scrupulous authors might test their recipes and perhaps tweak them in some way, or update them. One thirteenth-century Baghdad cookbook was expanded by adding 240 more recipes and in the process nearly all the original recipes were slightly rewritten to accommodate the reviser's taste or that of his time. When the original book was translated into Turkish two centuries later, the recipes were revised again.

There is a good deal of overlap between *Scents and Flavors* and the other major thirteenth-century cookbooks from the eastern Arab world, *Kitāb Waṣf al-aṭʿimah* and *Kanz al-fawāʾid*. A number of the shared recipes can be identified as coming from two eleventh-century medical encyclopedias, Ibn Sīnā's *Qānūn al-Ṭibb* and Ibn Jazlah's *Minhāj al-Bayān*. The authors of the encyclopedias presumably obtained the recipes from cooks, merely vetting them for their supposed medical value. Since the doctors considered the recipes to be in effect prescriptions, they were more precisely written than usual, so cookbook authors eagerly plagiarized them, though they didn't always bother to copy the medical information. (One collection from *Minhāj* that did include the medical material was translated into Latin in the fourteenth century as *Liber de Ferculis*.)

We know that *Scents and Flavors* was compiled in Syria at some time around the middle of the thirteenth century. Eventually two main text traditions diverged. Text Family A added a handful of recipes while Text Family B added 62 recipes, several written in a style quite different from the rest of the book. If this were all there were to the story, the picture of *Scents and Flavors* would be rather simple. However, one manuscript Ṣināʿah 74, does not fit into either Text Family A or B, though it is somewhat closer to A. It is clearly quite early, but it is also a mess. It appears to consist of at least two partial manuscripts bound together in only approximately the right place. At least four very different scribal hands can be distinguished. The chapter organization is wildly different from other versions and nearly all the recipes differ from the text as it appears in the other manuscripts; generally they are shorter and worded differently. Only in the pickles section are recipes numbered throughout, while numbers appear sporadically in the sweets chapter, suggesting that the scribes were working from a numbered text but simply shirked the job of writing the numbers, content to write "Another recipe. Another. Another." Large sections of the book give the feeling that the scribes were not copying a manuscript at all but transcribing recipes being read aloud to them, which would explain the abbreviated and sometimes jumbled nature of the text.

In short, Ṣināʿah 74 has the air of a particularly cheap and hasty edition of the book. On the other hand, its recipes, brief as they are, sometimes include wording that casts light on puzzles in the other manuscripts, so its recipes may represent an earlier stage of the text, tantalizingly beyond our grasp. But would this hypothetical earlier stage have been the author's original text or one related to it in some other way?

Indeed, the book's authorship is a mystery. Maxime Rodinson considered the issue at length in a 1948 essay "Études sur Manuscrits Arabes Rélatifs à la Cuisine." He noted that the manuscript at the Khuda Bakhsh Oriental Library in Bankipore, India, and a five-page fragment in Berlin ascribe it to one Kamāl al-Dīn Abū l-Qāsim ʿUmar al-Ḥalabī ibn al-ʿAdīm, likely the well-known Aleppo historian of the same name (1192–1262). To complicate matters, a manuscript formerly held at the library of the al-Ḥajjiyyāt School in Mosul ascribes it to a certain Jamāl al-Dīn Yaḥyā ibn al-ʿAẓīm al-Jazzār.

Rodinson suggested that the compiler was either the historian Ibn al-ʿAdīm, who adapted a preexisting anonymous work, or perhaps an unnamed Ayyubid prince who is fond of name-dropping the noble houses from which he obtained his recipes. Or perhaps the two men worked together, or that one of them wrote the core and the other rewrote it.[3] The manuscripts that have come to light since 1948 complicate the issue further. Lām 5076 ascribes it to al-Malik al-Saʿīd ibn Abī l-Jaysh, conceivably the Mamluk sultan Barakah Khān al-Saʿīd Nāṣir al-Dīn, who ruled 1279–90, making him rather younger than Ibn al-ʿAdīm, but he could not have been the prince who learned recipes from early thirteenth-century Ayyubid households. It is not out of the question, though, that a sultan would compile a recipe collection. Anecdotes in *The Meadows of Gold*, al-Masʿūdī's tenth-century anthology of entertaining lore, make it clear that an acquaintance with cuisine was at times held to be an important accomplishment in court circles, as it had been in Sassanid Persia. A late miscellany of recipes excerpted from *Scents and Flavors* at the Yazma ve Eski Basma Kütüphanesi in the old Inebey Medrese in Bursa, Turkey, ascribes that book to "the illustrious chief sheikh of Hama," though most manuscripts do not name an author at all.

Note on the Text

The present volume is the first translation of *Scents and Flavors* into any language. Paragraphing has been added according to Library of Arabic Literature style, and footnotes used in cases where an error, omissions, or uncertainty in the text obscures the instructions—otherwise they are used sparingly with a view to making the recipes clear and perhaps even usable in the kitchen. Names of recipes and dishes have been naturalized into untransliterated English wherever possible and feasible. Measurements have been translated where the equivalents are known. I have defined every Arabic term and unfamiliar item in a comprehensive Glossary at the back of the book.

As has been mentioned, recipes have disappeared or been added in every manuscript of *Scents and Flavors*. Fifteen recipes absent in the Topkapı manuscript on which this translation is based and other members of Text Family A seem to have appeared when the text was in an earlier state, to judge by their numbering and details of their wording. These "orphans" have been included here, and asterisked to indicate that they do not appear in the Topkapı manuscript on which this translation is based.

Text Family B adds 62 recipes from various sources. These are of considerable interest, both in themselves and as part of the larger tradition of this book, and are available online.

Many recipes end with a stock phrase, such as "It is tasty" or "It turns out nicely." In some cases these contribute to our understanding, but usually they are simply a way to signal that the recipe has ended, since medieval manuscripts do not have our convention of the paragraph break. This was a convenience for the reader, and also for the scribe, because it could provide some insurance against carelessly skipping several words and fusing two recipes together (a thing that sometimes did happen, to the confusion of later generations). In more expensively copied manuscripts, the tagline would alert the scribe to leave space for the title of the following recipe to be written later in red ink.

Often a recipe will list several ingredients of the same sort, such as "sugar and honey," "olive oil and fat," or "vinegar and lemon juice." In cases where there can be no doubt that "and" (*wa*) is an error for "or" (*aw*), it has been corrected. In other cases where it is not so clear, "and" has been left, but the reader should bear in mind that the recipe may be offering an option, not giving an order. The reader may also wish to bear in mind that the verbs "to lower" (*nazzala*) and "to leave" (*taraka*) could easily be confused by scribes when they were being rather casual about putting the appropriate dots above or below letters.

Notes to the Introduction

1 Dictionaries often suggest that it was a rice pudding, though few recipes recorded in the medieval cookbooks are based on rice.

2 This section on cold dishes might originally have stood as a chapter on its own, which is how it appears in the manuscript Ṣināʿah 74. It begins with the sort of heading that might begin a chapter.

3 Somewhat tenuously, Rodinson proposes that al-Jazzār's name might appear on the Mosul manuscript because he might have written his own book by the same title.

Scents and Flavors

In the name of God, the merciful and compassionate.
Help me, Lord, to complete my task well.

Praise to the one God, the Creator, guarantor of our livelihood, 0.1
Who deserves our whole-hearted praise. May this prayer suffice to elicit His generous provision and evince our gratitude for the blessings He has bestowed upon us. In honor of human beings, He has said, «For sustenance, We have provided them with things good and pure, and exalted them over many of Our creatures.»[1] Praise to Him for reproaching those who would forbid good sustenance to His servants, as He does in the verse: «Say: "Who has forbidden the adornment of God, which He has brought forth for His servants, and good things, clean and pure, which God has provided for them?" Say: "Those good things are lawful for the believers in the present life and shall be exclusively for them on the Day of Resurrection."»[2]

In revealing His will in His noble Book, the Almighty shows His generosity to His creation, saying, «It is He who has made the earth subservient to you, so traverse its regions and eat its provisions.»[3]

He sent Muḥammad, blessings and peace be upon him, who declared Him to be One when others said He was part of a trinity. Through him God showed how to render judgment in all circumstances, He being the One «who commands them to do right and forbids them to do wrong, who makes good things lawful for them and bad things unlawful.»[4]

God favored him with the largest share of every good thing and made him love the beauty of women and the fragrance of perfume.

I pray for God's peace and blessing upon him, the blessing of the most noble Lover upon the most distinguished of beloveds.

0.2 The greater part of the pleasures of this life and the next involves the consumption of tempting food and drink. Similarly, perfuming one's body and clothing endears one to one's friends, male or female, and has therefore become customary, when dressing up, dining, sampling scents, or drinking. What is more, consuming good foods strengthens adoration in God's servants and draws pure praise from their hearts. It is for these reasons that God's grace in bestowing these blessings is repeatedly mentioned in His noble Book, where they are accorded praise and distinction.

For these reasons, too, I have compiled this book, which I have titled *Scents and Flavors the Banqueter Savors*. I have included nothing without having tested it repeatedly, eaten it copiously, having worked the recipe out for myself, and tasted and touched it personally. I begin with perfume, because it is honored greatly, reputed highly, and celebrated widely. Thereafter I set forth the sections according to an order which, as you proceed, you will see clearly. I hope through God's generosity to achieve as reward the best of fates. I ask God the Exalted to make what I have written here useful. He is near and answers our prayers, truly.

Chapter 1

Perfume

Section on *ʿanbarīnā* with musk

Knead musk with gum tragacanth soaked in willow water and form into apple shapes, as you would ambergris. The willow water makes it pungent. Do not add rose water or the scent will be weakened. 1.1

A second variety, better than the first, and with a more pungent aroma Scrape agarwood with rose water on a sandalwood stone. When you accumulate a good amount, squeeze dry in a cloth and transfer it to a bowl. Scrape Maqasiri sandalwood, as you did the agarwood, making two equal portions. Mix everything and knead with rose water in a china vessel. Spread the mixture thinly in the vessel and smoke several times over agarwood and several times over ambergris. Between every two or three fumigations, sprinkle with rose water, shape, spread out as before, and smoke again. When it is done, put on a little civet and musk, and let dry in the vessel. Knead with gum tragacanth soaked in rose water and make into apple shapes, as above. Sprinkle with rose water and smoke as soon as cut for use. This makes for a more pungent aroma. 1.2

A different sandalwood *ʿanbarīnā*, worn in summer and in hot weather to cool the humors Scrape Maqasiri sandalwood with rose water, shape, and spread out in a china bowl. 1.3

Smoke five times with ambergris, shape it with gum tragacanth dissolved with rose water and musk, and make into *ʿanbarīnā*. It is the best.

◆

1.4 **AGARWOOD** Split and soak in rose water for seven days. This will make its aroma pungent.

1.5 **ELEVATED AGARWOOD** Split the agarwood. Dissolve sugar crystals with rose water and cook into a thick syrup, the consistency of thickened oxymel. Put in ambergris kneaded with a little musk and wait patiently for the ambergris to melt. Add the agarwood and stir until the syrup coats it. Set aside and dry in the open air. Take care not to overcook the syrup; it should remain liquid. This kind has a surpassing aroma.

1.6 **A BETTER ELEVATED AGARWOOD PREPARATION** Split the agarwood, soak in rose water for seven days, and let dry. Grind sugar crystals fine. Put a tray on the fire and in it melt raw ambergris and ambergris paste along with a little musk. When melted, add the sugar and stir. Once everything is mixed, put in the agarwood and stir until the ambergris coats it thoroughly. It will turn white and give off a good aroma in the incense burner.

1.7 **AN INCENSE OF THE KIND MADE FOR IBN BARMAK—HEALTHFUL DURING THE CHANGE OF SEASONS AND IN DAMP WEATHER** Take two *mithqāl*s of nutmeg, a *mithqāl* each of roses, spikenard, clove, mastic, saffron, and liquid storax, half a *mithqāl* each of brown cardamom, cubeb, and camphor, and a *dāniq* of musk. Pound, knead with rose water, and form into tablets. Dry out and use.

1.8 ***NADD* INCENSE TABLETS OF THE KIND MADE FOR IBN AL-AGHLAB** One *mithqāl* each of camphor, both sweet and bitter costus, ambergris, labdanum, liquid storax, and tree moss, and two *mithqāls* of saffron, a quarter *mithqāl* of fragrant shell, and a *mithqāl* of agarwood. Pound everything, sift it, and knead with the ben oil from which *ghāliyah* perfume is made, and make into tablets.

NADD INCENSE TABLETS OF THE KIND MADE FOR CALIPHS Ten dirhams of raw agarwood, two dirhams each of costus and fragrant shell, two dirhams of musked *sukk* incense pastilles, and one-half plus one-third dirham of camphor. Pound, sieve, and knead with rose water. Melt a quarter *mithqāl* of ambergris in this, form into tablets, and let them dry. It is used for smoking things. 1.9

A GOOD YEMENI WINTER INCENSE FOR USE ON ALL FURS EXCEPT SQUIRREL Two parts agarwood, one and a half parts Maqasiri sandalwood, and half a part each of sweet costus, bitter costus, and fragrant shell. Pound everything, smashing the agarwood and sandalwood into small pieces. Boil the fragrant shell, clean the fat and dirt with a knife, then pound. Take half a part each of dry green myrtle and orange peel, and pound also. Take rose water, dissolve sugar and honey in it, and make a thick syrup. Add ambergris-like labdanum, ambergris paste, and saffron. Mix the ingredients; stir until thoroughly mixed. Transfer to a tray and spread out to cool. Add a quarter *mithqāl* of civet. 1.10

A VERY AGREEABLE BARMAKIYYAH INCENSE, USEFUL FOR PERFUMING THOSE WHO HAVE BEEN IN VESTIBULES AND REST ROOMS Take one part each of sweet costus, bitter costus, and fragrant shell, two *ūqiyahs* of snipped dry myrtle and ambergris-like labdanum twisted small, and one-half part each dried orange peel, saffron threads, and dried lemon peel. Pound everything. Dissolve honey with rose water and wine vinegar, and thicken on the fire, putting in a good quantity of ambergris-like labdanum and saffron, until it has a good consistency. Add the pounded ingredients, stir, and spread out in the shade to dry. 1.11

1.12 ***NADD* INCENSE WICKS** Put vine-shoot charcoal or quince fuzz—charcoal is better—in good triple-refined ambergris and make into wicks. When you want to smoke something, light and then extinguish them—they will produce good smoke. I have seen wicks placed together with a stick of agarwood in plum-shaped containers of pierced, finely wrought silver and left in a person's pocket. The smoke is long-lasting, suffusing everything from the pocket most agreeably.

1.13 **A RECIPE FOR INCENSE CAKES** Six or seven[5] dirhams of Qaqulli agarwood, three dirhams of Maqasiri sandalwood, a *mithqāl* of ambergris paste, half a *mithqāl* of raw ambergris, a quarter *mithqāl* of musk, a quarter dirham of dry lemon peel, the same each of orange peel, clove, and mace, and half a dirham of saffron. Pound everything a bit coarsely. Take six dirhams of sugar crystals, add ten dirhams of refined white sugar, and make a syrup with Nisibin rose water; boil to a thick consistency. Add in all the ingredients along with a quarter dirham of civet and spread the mixture out in a tray. When cool, rub with a pounding stone until no bit sticks to another. Take psyllium seed and soak in rose water. When soaked, extract the mucilage through a cloth and knead the ingredients with it. Form into cakes and place on a sieve to dry. Make sure the rose-water syrup is not too thin—it should have the thickness of brittle *ʿaqīd*, or be thicker.

1.14 **ANOTHER KIND OF INCENSE CAKE** Pound finely and sift one and a sixth dirhams each of citron peel, sour-orange peel, pomelo peel, Fathi apple peel, and myrtle. Sift two *mithqāl*s each of Qamari agarwood and Maqasiri sandalwood, one *mithqāl* each of ambergris-like labdanum, mastic, saffron threads, camphor, quince fuzz, and costus, and two *mithqāl*s of ambergris. Take sugar crystals and make them into a thick syrup with rose water, willow water, and clove water. Make it extremely thick as described above. Add the ingredients, form into cakes, set on a sieve to dry, then use.

BARMAKIYYAH INCENSE Three quarters of an *ūqiyah* of agarwood, half an *ūqiyah* of Maqasiri sandalwood, half an *ūqiyah* of hearts of sweet costus which have been soaked in rose water, peeled, and dried in the shade, half an *ūqiyah* of musk, a sixth of an *ūqiyah* of ground saffron, a dirham of mastic, half a dirham of Qurashi fragrant shell, a dirham of fresh labdanum, the same of pure pomegranate juice, and a quarter *mithqāl* of Ribahi camphor. Pound everything and sift.[6] Dissolve the labdanum with rose water on a low fire, boil, add to the pounded ingredients, and leave to infuse each other. Then take one part juice of ripe Damascus apples and one-half part *nammām*, knead together, and mix with other ingredients. After kneading, grind the camphor, add to the ingredients, and allow to mature overnight. Make into tablets of any shape you want and dry on a sieve. The smoke is used to perfume things. 1.15

ANOTHER BARMAKIYYAH INCENSE RECIPE Pound a quarter *ūqiyah* of mature dark agarwood, half an *ūqiyah* of Maqasiri sandalwood, a quarter *ūqiyah* of peeled sweet costus soaked in rose water and then dried, a quarter dirham of mastic, half a dirham of Qurashi fragrant shell, three quarters of a dirham of ground saffron, a quarter dirham of fresh labdanum, and a quarter dirham of pomegranate juice. Sift and knead with three quarters of a dirham of apple juice, *nammām* juice, and honey. Knead, form into balls, and dry. 1.16

***NADD* COMPOUNDED FOR INCENSE** A quarter *ūqiyah* of Indian agarwood, a quarter *mithqāl*[7] of aromatic musked *sukk* pastilles, half a *mithqāl* of saffron, a *mithqāl* of fatty ambergris, half a *mithqāl* of musk, a quarter *mithqāl* of Ribahi camphor, and a quarter *mithqāl* of fresh labdanum. Grind everything except the ambergris, musk, and camphor. Knead firm and dry with the juice of fresh Damascus apples, *nammām*, and marjoram—twice as much apple juice as *nammām*. Let ripen for a day and a night. Then form the ambergris into small cakes, heat a tray, and throw them on. When the ambergris softens, add skimmed white honey and put in the labdanum 1.17

with the ambergris as well. When the ambergris runs, remove it from the fire, add the aromatic ingredients, and knead as firmly as possible. Then take everything out, place on a stone slab rubbed with rose water, and grind with a pounding stone moistened with rose water until smooth. When everything is thoroughly mixed, remove and spread out on marble. Cut into pieces of any shape desired, and leave on a sieve for fifteen days some place where the air is free of dust.

If you want to boil this with ambergris, take ambergris and dissolve it in a tray on a low fire. Put in the pieces, turn them over, return them to the sieve, and leave until they dry and harden.

Section on powders

1.18 Pound an *ūqiyah* of spikenard fine and sieve. Pound a dirham each of clove and mace, dissolve with rose water, and spread out in a porcelain bowl. Smoke the mixture three times over Yemeni incense, seven times over agarwood, and five times over ambergris. Every two or three times, turn the bowl over, knead the mixture, and spray with rose water. The better you smoke it, the better it will smell. When you make it into cakes, add a dirham of civet. Put the cakes in a sieve to dry in the shade, then grind, add five dirhams' weight of crushed ambergris along with musk, and put in a vessel. It has a pleasing smell.

1.19 **A warming powder** An *ūqiyah* of spikenard, a quarter *ūqiyah* of cloves, five dirhams of cardamom, and three dirhams of mace. Pound the ingredients, dissolve with rose water, and smoke as described in the preceding recipe. It helps coldness of the head and fortifies the brain.

1.20 **A cooling powder** Scrape Maqasiri sandalwood on a stone together with rose water, then squeeze out the rose water using a cloth. Spread out the sandalwood in a bowl and smoke it several times with agarwood and ambergris. Add a *mithqāl* of musk and ambergris and a quarter dirham of civet, and it is ready for use.

CYPERUS POWDER Pound one part cyperus, one part Qamari agarwood, and one part Maqasiri sandalwood, and sieve. Knead with rose water and dry in the shade. When dry, pound again, knead with rose water, and dry; repeat three times. When dry, pound and add a *dāniq* each of camphor and musk for every ten dirhams' weight. 1.21

CITRON POWDER Ten dirhams of cinnamon bark, a *mithqāl* of tree moss, two *mithqāls* of sandalwood, and the zest of a citron. Pound the first ingredients fine, then pound with the citron zest until everything is entirely mixed. Knead with rose water, and smoke with costus and agarwood, seven times each. Dry, pound smooth, and it is ready to use. 1.22

ROSE POWDER Fifteen dirhams of rose hips, a *mithqāl* of Qamari agarwood, three dirhams of Maqasiri sandalwood, and a dirham of brown cardamom. Pound and sieve everything. Knead with rose water and smoke five times with costus, fragrant shell, and sandalwood. Then smoke with agarwood six or seven times, kneading it every two or three fumigations as before. Dry and grind, and it is ready to use. 1.23

AN AROMATIC POWDER Equal quantities of spikenard, betel nut, clove, nutmeg, bay leaf, cardamom, mace, cultivated rose hips removed from the stems, both sweet and bitter costus, and tree moss. Pound and sieve fine. Soak psyllium seed with rose water and extract its mucilage through a cloth. Knead with the ingredients, make into large cakes, and stick them on the inside of a new earthenware pot. Then take sugar crystals, Qamari agarwood, sandalwood, fragrant shell boiled and cleaned of fat, ambergris-like labdanum, sweet costus, bitter costus, sour-orange peel, myrtle leaves cut up 1.24

with scissors, *bizr* seeds, mastic, and saffron threads. Pound and put in the bottom of another small pot; the ingredients should be in equal quantities. Overturn the pot with the incense cakes stuck in it onto the small pot and seal the two rims together with clay so that no fumes or aromas escape. Put the pot with the incense on a low fire for a whole night and a whole day. Make sure that the fire is not hot enough to burn the incense, but low, so that it smokes. When the incense is consumed, open the pot, remove the incense cakes, and dry them in the shade. Grind fine and add ambergris, ground agarwood, a little musk, and a little civet.

1.25 **AN INCOMPARABLE ANTIPERSPIRANT** A hundred dirhams of *marāzibī* zinc oxide, fifteen dirhams of violets, and seven dirhams of tree moss. Soak the moss in rose water for a day, then squeeze dry and pound to bits. Put everything in a mortar and pour in the rose water in which the moss was soaked; if more is needed, plain rose water will do. Beat until dry. Add rose water and beat as described five times more. When ready, leave in a glass vessel until dried to the point that it will stick to a porcelain bowl. Smoke the bowl ten times with agarwood, then ten times with ambergris. Knead between every two fumigations, then stick to the bowl again, and spray with rose water. When sufficiently smoked, grind to a fine dust and then use. This powder prevents underarm odor and perfumes the breath. It is the best recipe for this, so there is no need to describe any others.

Section on fragrant oils

1.26 Take almond oil mixed with rose petals. Smoke cotton and pour the rose almond oil on. (To smoke cotton, take fine cotton and card it. Grease a porcelain vessel, stick the cotton inside and smoke with agarwood and ambergris six or seven times.) Pour on almond oil, sprinkle with ambergris and musk, and it is ready to use.

SMOKED OIL, KNOWN AS STINK OIL—GOOD FOR COLD WINDS, BLOATING, PHLEGMATIC SWELLINGS, CATARRH, AND SWELLINGS IN THE FINGERS; IT CUTS RANCID ODOR, AND IS KNOWN ONLY TO A FEW Take one part each of nutmeg, cardamom, Indian mace, clove, spikenard, betel nut, bay leaves, and clove. Likewise take two parts cultivated rosehips removed from their stems and the same of tree moss. Pound everything together, sieve into a *khātūniyyah* mortar, and grind well. Mix with ambergris and ground Maqasiri sandalwood; mix and grind everything. This is the powder part of the recipe. Then take three parts agarwood, two parts sugar crystals, one part each of sweet costus, bitter costus, and Maqasiri sandalwood, and a fragrant shell dissolved in henna. Knead with it and leave overnight. In the morning, boil the mixture. Clean one and one-half parts ambergris-like labdanum twisted into small pieces, one part dry myrtle leaves clipped with scissors and one part saffron threads. Crush in a mortar; this is the incense part. Then take cotton and card finely. Grease a large bowl with fresh sesame oil and stick the cotton in, leaving the bottom without any cotton, or it will burn. Put two or three burning coals on a tray and put a good bit of the incense on. Turn the bowl with the cotton stuck inside over it and smoke; when that incense is used up, smoke again. Then turn the piece of cotton over and stick onto the bowl as described, and as before. Spray a little light sesame oil on and smoke seven times, then smoke with ambergris. When the cotton turns yellow, sprinkle well with the powder described above and put in enough fresh sesame oil to cover by a little. If you have ben oil available, all the better; put the cotton and sesame oil in it. Sprinkle with as much musk and civet as you can, and it is ready to use. You can also add to the powder some tree moss—not ground—and rose petals. 1.27

AN OIL OF MINE WHICH BENEFITS COLD PHLEGMATIC WINDS, COLDNESS OF THE HEAD, AND BACK PAIN Take spikenard, betel nut, cloves, fresh laurel leaves, nutmeg, mace, cardamom, tree 1.28

moss, rose-infused oil, rosehips, both sweet and bitter costus, and saffron threads. Pound and sieve everything. Extract the mucilage of psyllium seeds with clove water and rose water. Take the mucilage and knead a round piece with it, and put it in the bottom of a greased jar. Pour in enough oil to fill the jar. Then take sweet and bitter costus, labdanum, sandalwood, mastic, myrtle leaves, sour-orange peel, saffron threads, agarwood, sandarac resin, and pieces of frankincense, and put all in a small jar, the mouth of which will fit into the mouth of the larger jar. Plug its mouth with a bunch of myrtle and a bunch of basil to keep the incense from falling out, then overturn into the mouth of the other jar, making sure that the oil does not reach it, and seal the joint with clay. Dig a small hole, bury the larger jar in the hole up to the bottom of the jug, and pile dirt around it and on the bottom of the small jar, leaving a little uncovered. Build a good fire over it for two days and nights. When the incense, myrtle, and basil are consumed, take out the ingredients in the bottom of the jar, form into balls, and use. When you plug the top of the jar, plug it tightly, so that when the herbs burn, they don't fall into the oil and spoil it.

1.29 **RECIPE FOR EXTRACTING BEN OIL, WHICH FEW DO WELL** Take moringa seeds, peel, and grind on querns like the querns used for the seeds known in Damascus as *jalājil*.[8] When ground, put in a big copper pot with a capacity of ten *kaylajah*s by Damascus measure. If you can't find a quern, pound the seeds in a regular or a large stone mortar until they swim in their oil. Put enough in a pot to fill a third and pour water to cover by four spread fingers' width. Kindle a fire underneath with plenty of heavy wood until it boils. Cook for half a day, adding water whenever the level goes down, until midday, then stop feeding the fire and leave to cool and to go out. Then remove the oil risen to the top of the vessel until none is left. Throw away the dregs and hulls together with their water, put the oil in a vessel to settle, and filter off the clear part.

If you want to cook it with spices, the method is as follows. Aḥmad ibn Yaʿqūb, the client of the son of al-ʿAbbās, said he puts the ben oil described above in big soapstone pots and cooks it with the same amount of pure water until the water evaporates. He does this three times, then he cooks the oil with rose water and pounded, sieved yellow Maqasiri sandalwood until the water evaporates. Next he cooks it with rose water and Indian agarwood for two days and with good ground musk dissolved with rose water for a day. Then he removes it from the fire and takes the clear part. He puts in Tibetan musk dissolved with rose water and cooks until it evaporates. This is fine ben oil, used in *ghāliyah* perfume. 1.30

AS FOR BEN OIL COOKED WITH SPICES it is not good for making *ghāliyah*, because the smell of the spices overwhelms the smell of the musk and ambergris. The recipe is Ceylon cinnamon, clove, grain of paradise, spikenard, and mace. Pound everything, put in a big vessel, and pour on hot water for two days and nights. Bring to the boil several times after it is done, strain, and put into the ben oil. Boil the ben oil on a low fire tor two days and nights until the water evaporates. When it evaporates, take Maqasiri sandalwood, soak in rose water, and boil until its essence comes out. Strain and put on the ben oil, and boil until the water evaporates and ben oil remains. Then take best Indian agarwood, pound, boil with the oil and rose water until the rose water goes away and only the oil is left, and remove. 1.31

ANOTHER RECIPE FOR SPICED BEN OIL Take a *mann* of brown Chinese cinnamon in thin sticks for every ten *mann*s of the oil. Boil enough hot water to more than cover, and bury the vessel in hot ashes so that no vapors escape. Leave for a day and a night. Boil on a good fire, strain the water onto the ben oil, and boil the oil until the water is gone. Take three quarters of a *mann* of pulverized brown *tuffāḥi* cinnamon and soak in hot water for a day and a night. Strain and boil with the oil that was cooked with the Chinese cinnamon; boil until 1.32

the water evaporates. Then take three-quarters of a *mann* of Ceylon cinnamon and clove, and crush them. Boil ten *mann*s of water, pour on them, bury, and leave for two days and nights. Then bring to a boil, strain onto the oil, and cook half a day so that the water evaporates, leaving the oil. Then take a quarter of a *mann* of Ceylon cinnamon and cloves and crush thoroughly. Boil ten *mann*s of water and pour hot onto the cloves and bury it for two days and nights. Strain it onto the ben oil and boil until the water evaporates, leaving the oil. Then take four *mann*s of brown mace, soak in hot water for a day and a night, strain the water onto the oil, and cook until the water boils off, leaving the oil. Next take rose hips and pour ten *mann*s of hot water on them and bury for two days, strain onto the oil, and boil until it dries. Then take half a *mann* of *ʿaṣāfīrī* spikenard cleaned of its fluff, slivers, stems, and dirt. Take ten *mann*s of water, boil, and bury with the oil for two days, and boil it as described. Take half a *mann* of yellow Maqasiri sandalwood, mince on a leather mat and put in a vessel. Boil ten *mann*s of water, add, and bury for two days and nights. Then boil, strain onto the oil, and boil again until the water goes away. Next take a quarter *mann* of the best-quality agarwood, soak for three days in water brought to the boil, boil, and strain onto the oil. Pour some more water on the agarwood, boil a great deal, strain on the oil also, and cook until the water goes away. Then take half a *mithqāl* of Tibetan musk and grind four *mithqāl*s of musk-enriched *sukk* pastilles; bolt them through a piece of silk, knead with pungent rose water, dissolve with rose water to the consistency of thin soup, and pour onto the oil in a fresh soapstone pot on a low fire of embers. As it boils, stir continuously with a length of reed until the rose water boils away. The sign that it has dried sufficiently is that the musk and musked *sukk* cling to the end of the reed like *ghāliyah* perfume. Remove from the fire and allow to cool. Bottle the clear part for use. If you want to reduce the inconvenience, gather the ingredients, or as many of them as you want, into the waters, boil, pour onto the oil, and boil until the water evaporates, after having pounded and crushed the dry ingredients.

Chapter 2

Beverages

YEMENI *SŪBIYYAH* Make white sugar into as thin a syrup as possible. Take best-quality wheat flour and make a thick porridge without any salt. Let cool, transfer to a basin, and beat by hand. Ladle on syrup—not all at once, but ladle by ladle—until it acquires the consistency of thick flour soup. The more you beat it, the frothier it will be. Pour on shaken-up saddlebag fruit beer;[9] in Egypt, they use spiced oxymel instead. Once it is diluted, transfer to a used vessel, such as one with a trace of fruit molasses or honey. Put in a lot of rue tied in bundles, as well as mint, mixed spices, rose water, and musk—and don't skimp on the spices. Put in a warm place, and cover with a large wide lid; the mixture will turn foamy. When the foam is absorbed, shake in some more fruit beer, and it is ready to drink. The proportion of ingredients is not spelled out here—you decide sweetness, plainness, and spiciness based on desired taste. Also, when the foam rises, you can smoke a glass vessel or a Yemeni *ḥuqq* with agarwood and ambergris, put the *sūbiyyah* in it, and it is ready to use. 2.1

A VARIATION Use the same recipe, but add rice and boil. It becomes a different kind of dish—you slurp the *sūbiyyah* and eat the rice. Some people make it with rice flour, but top-quality wheat flour is better. The more you beat it, the better the foam will be. 2.2

2.3 **YEMENI *SHISHSH*** Take flour, cook into a thick porridge, and sprinkle with saddlebag fruit beer. Sweeten with honey or sugar and put in fresh orange peels, mint, rue, mixed spices, and special fruit beer yeast, and let it get warm. Place it in straw or a warm room until foam rises, and it is ready to drink.

2.4 ***ANOTHER PREPARATION** Cook two quarts of rice and half a quart of white flour in water until the rice disintegrates. Strain through a wheat-flour sieve, add enough sugar and honey to sweeten the taste, and throw in a piece of sourdough. Pour in five small jugs of fruit-flavored beer with some musk and rose water. Put in a new jug—either new or used—and seal with orange blossoms. Bury in straw for half a day. It is then ready for consumption.

2.5 **RECONSTITUTED POMEGRANATE—GOOD FOR NAUSEA AND VOMITING, AND STIMULATES THE APPETITE** Soak two parts dried pomegranate seeds in lily water, borage water, and rose water. Add mint and rue, squeeze fresh lemons over, and sweeten with sugar. It is better than fruit beer, which impairs intercourse and digestion.

2.6 **SUGAR AND LEMON DRINK** White sugar, lily water, mixed spices, and borage water. Crumble rue and mint into the mixture, and spray with rose water and fresh lemon juice. Pour into a flask smoked with ambergris. This is better for you than fruit beer.

2.7 **MARINATED SWEET-KERNELED APRICOT DRINK** Wash dried sweet-kerneled apricots, pour lily water, borage water, and a little rose water on them, and squeeze on some sour pomegranate juice. Add mint and sweeten with sugar; leave the apricots to soak. Nothing is more aromatic, delightful, and good for the health.

2.8 **SWEET-KERNELED APRICOT SNACKS** Dissolve sugar in rose water and musk with a little water and soak dried apricots in it, but not so much that they disintegrate. Remove the apricots and dry in a clean spot. This is one of the best and most delightful snacks there is.

PREPARED POMEGRANATE SEEDS Pound two parts pomegranate seeds fine and add one part white sugar and mint leaves, sweetening with the sugar as you pound. Spray with rose water, pound, and smoke with ambergris two or three times, and it is ready to use.[10] 2.9

SOUR ORANGE DRINK Remove the pulp and cook the juice as for the citron drink. It is intense. 2.10

A CURE FOR NAUSEA Take lemon juice, fresh sour pomegranate juice, local rose water, sour grape juice, strained juice of soaked and macerated tamarind, wine vinegar, and the reconstituted juice of dried pomegranate seeds. Add sugar and thicken on the fire. Stir along with two bunches of mint and put in pieces of quince and mixed spices. Take fresh lemons, boil, split in four, stuff with pepper and mixed spices, and put them in the syrup until done, having squeezed into it some of the water they were boiled in. Thicken to the consistency of electuaries and add pieces of agarwood. When one bunch of mint wilts, replace it with the other. This makes for an excellent drink. 2.11

CITRON DRINK Peel citrons and take their sour flesh as whole pulp. Sprinkle with sugar, and add sour orange juice, borage water, lily water, rose water, and willow water. 2.12

There is a variation to the above recipe, by adding rue and some mixed spices—it is quite tasty. Pomelo can be similarly used. 2.13

SPICED OXYMEL Take a used vessel and put bread crumbs of white *kumāj* bread in it. Pour on hot water and some special fruit-beer yeast and leave overnight. Then stir carefully and strain in such a way that you do not macerate or touch the bread at all. Take the clear part of the liquid and strain through a fine filter. Sweeten with 2.14

sugar and add rue, mint, and mixed spices: specifically, just ginger, cardamom, and a little clove but not the rest of the usual spices, because they would blacken it. Add some rose water. Remove the bread from the vessel and put the oxymel back in, leave to rise, and it is ready to use. If you are some place where bread is not available, use pounded biscuits, or cook up a soup thickened with flour and use instead.

2.15 **QUINCES COOKED WITH SUGAR** Take *qaṣabī* quinces. Split, remove the cores, and boil in water. Make a thin syrup, add the quinces, and cook continuously on a low fire until the syrup becomes thick and red, acquiring the color of carnelian, and the quinces are properly done. Whenever any are done, take them out, until it is nearly time to take the pot from the fire, then put them back in. When you use both *qaṣabī* and *barzī* quinces, the *barzī* ones will fall apart and spoil. Add fresh lemon juice if you want to make it sour. If you pound some of the quinces and take their filtered juice and add to the syrup, it becomes very strong. When you remove it from the fire, add rose water, musk, raw ambergris, and Qaqulli agarwood.

Chapter 3

How to Make Various Kinds of Fruit Juices and Treat Them, How to Distill Vinegar

sour grape juice Take unripe sour grapes, picking from the bunches, and squeeze in a press. If you do not have a press, pound them in a large wooden bowl with a stone and squeeze by hand until nothing remains on the peels. Then pour the juice into a new tinned pot and leave overnight to settle. Put the juice on a hot fire and bring to the boil. If you have grape juice left over, add some to the pot whenever it boils down until the juice is all used up. Keep on boiling until it is boiled down by half and has the reddish-brown color of jujubes. Add pieces of Chinese cinnamon and stir with seven big bunches of mint, over and over; when one bunch wilts, stir with another. Take the pot from the fire and leave to settle and clear. When the juice is cold and the lees have settled out, transfer the clear part to a glass container. Fill and seal with sesame oil. If the vessel isn't full, put a cover on it. It absolutely must be sealed with either sesame or olive oil, but olive oil turns rancid, so sesame oil is better. I have kept sour grape juice six years without it spoiling because I cooked it properly. 3.1

sour grape juice of the sun Squeeze sour grapes into a vessel and strain. Put the juice in a glass container, set out in the sun until 3.2

it reduces, and it is ready to use. It is not very good, but I describe it for the sake of completeness.

3.3 **LEMON JUICE—FOR DRINKING** After washing lemons by hand, squeeze them onto chunks of sugar. Put the juice in a glass vessel and use in beverages when required.

3.4 **SOUR ORANGE JUICE—A RARITY, OF WHICH MOST PEOPLE HAVE NEVER HEARD** Put a little salt in a glass vessel. Take sour oranges and have one person peel them and another squeeze; the one who peels should not squeeze, or the juice will be bitter. When the oranges have been squeezed, leave the juice to settle. Take the clear part, add stems of rue, and put in the sun. It is the most delicious drink one can imagine.

3.5 **RECIPE FOR SOFTENING SOUR ORANGES** Arrange the oranges separately in rows in a high, airy place and leave for a week. Squeeze as before.

3.6 **SUMAC JUICE** Take sumac, pound the fruits, soak in a little water, then extract the juice through a piece of cloth and allow to clear. Use as needed.

3.7 **WHITE VINEGAR** Put mint in vinegar, pack into the still head, and distill on a low fire. It comes out as mint-flavored white vinegar.

3.8 **ANOTHER WHITE VINEGAR RECIPE** Knead the vinegar with bran, pack the still with it, and distill.

Chapter 4

How to Melt the Several Varieties of Tail Fat

THE FIRST Take fat lamb tail, chop small, and put on the fire. 4.1
Add two or three ladles of water and cook until partly melted. Add pieces of quince and Fathi apple, a handful of coriander seeds, a bunch of dill, and a peeled onion, and continue on a low fire until no tail is visible. Add pieces of Chinese cinnamon and salt. When the tail is done and turns brown, add mastic—but not until the tail has exuded all its fat, or it will prevent the fat from coming out and hold it in. When done, put through a strainer, leave to cool off, and store in a vessel.

If you want it to be yellow, like clarified butter, after the straining and before it solidifies, finely pound *wars* dye, boil, and add to the fat. This will color it yellow and improve its flavor. Make sure no water remains in the fat.

RED TAIL FAT Take rendered tail fat, add red sweet root,[11] and use. 4.2

GREEN TAIL FAT Take rendered tail fat and add some strained 4.3
chard puree.[12] Boil, strain, and it will turn green.[13]

4.4 Since "mixed spices" are repeatedly mentioned in this book, a detailed description is in order. They comprise a mixture of spikenard, betel nut, bay leaf, nutmeg, mace, cardamom, clove, rose hips, ash tree fruits, long pepper, ginger, and black pepper, all pounded separately.

Chapter 5

Chicken Dishes—Sweet, Sour, and Other Varieties

ROAST CHICKEN Take chickens and, before slaughtering them, exhaust them until they are too tired to fly or walk. Then slaughter and roast. Their meat is more tender than the meat of chickens that can walk. 5.1

SECOND RECIPE Put a fattened chicken on a skewer. Dig a niche in a wall and build a hot charcoal fire in it. Take sieved bread crumbs and place in a pan or tray under the chicken, but not on the fire. Roast in the niche on the side exposed to the fire, letting the fat drip onto the bread crumbs. When done, add sugar, pistachios, and rose water to the bread crumbs and stuff the chicken. While the chicken is roasting, rub with chicken fat, rose water, beaten sesame oil, and salt, keeping the pan or tray beneath it. From time to time, use a feather to baste the chicken with rose water and sesame oil. 5.2

THIRD RECIPE Take a chicken and roast until done. When done, put wine vinegar, enough pounded caraway, mint, and pounded garlic on it, and bring to the boil two or three times. It comes out well. 5.3

5.4 **FOURTH RECIPE** Hang the chicken in a clay oven as for roasting and rub it with saffron. Put rice and milk under it to cook as a *jūdhābah*. It is tasty.

5.5 **FIFTH RECIPE** Boil the chicken in water with just enough salt in it to taste. Stuff it, and rub it well with sesame oil.[14] When half done, put between two sheets of dough, making an opening two fingers wide at the head, and put in a brick oven. Watch attentively through that opening to tell how done it is. Feel the meat, and when done, remove and serve.

Section on bread-crumb stuffing, of which there are several varieties

5.6 **FIRST VARIETY** Take the sieved crumbs of white *kumāj* bread. Take three parts parsley, one part mint, and one-half part rue. Mince them all fine and rub with the bread crumbs until the herbs wilt. Add toasted pistachios crushed in a mortar, along with coriander seeds, caraway, thyme, mixed spices, pepper, salt, ground Chinese cinnamon, a bit of olive oil, and some toasted sesame oil. Knead with lemon juice until it is sour enough for you. Then boil a chicken and fry until done. Stuff with the bread-crumb mixture and spread some on the breast and wings and between the thighs. Then thin the remainder of the stuffing with just enough chicken broth and lemon juice that you can dip bread in it and pick some up, and place in a bowl. Use only a small amount of bread crumbs; the more pistachios, the better.

5.7 **SECOND VARIETY** Make the same bread-crumb mixture as described above, but add sugar.

5.8 **THIRD VARIETY** Or add sugar, sesame paste, vinegar, a little lemon juice, and garlic. There should be less vinegar than lemon juice. This is an outstanding dish.

FOURTH VARIETY Make as described with the addition of broth boiled on the fire with the chicken. This variation should have more bread crumbs than the others. 5.9

FIFTH VARIETY Put cooked chicken and pullets in a mixture of lemon juice, minced parsley, mint, rue, pistachios, pepper, coriander seeds, caraway, salt, and sugar. This variation does not contain any bread. For all these stuffing dishes, if you take the chicken livers and giblets, boil them, chop small, and fry, and put into the stuffing—inside the chicken, not on its back—you get a tasty dish. 5.10

SIXTH VARIETY Take lemon juice. Mince parsley, mint, and a little rue into it—not so much that it is no longer liquid—then add pounded pepper, coriander seeds, caraway, mixed spices, and pounded Chinese cinnamon. Fry the chicken and put into the stuffing while hot. Put it in the bowl and pour on a little of the broth. 5.11

A SIMILAR VARIATION Instead of lemon juice, use sour grape juice. 5.12

ANOTHER SIMILAR VARIATION Instead of sour grape juice, sour orange juice. 5.13

ANOTHER SIMILAR VARIATION Use vinegar, lemon juice, and sugar, with more lemon juice than vinegar. The herbs and spices remain the same. 5.14

SEVENTH VARIETY Pound sumac. Take the fruits and all and squeeze fresh lemon juice on it, or the juice of pickled lemons if fresh is unavailable, and soak for a while, then extract the juice through a cloth. Take toasted walnuts—or better yet, hazelnuts—pounded smooth, and crushed toasted pistachios. Take minced parsley, mint, rue, coriander seeds, caraway, a good deal of thyme, mixed spices, garlic, Chinese cinnamon, and sieved *kumāj* bread crumbs. Season the crumbs with mixed spices and parsley until the parsley wilts. 5.15

Add the pounded sumac along with the juice the sumac was soaking in. If it is too sour or if you need to dilute it, mix in some meat broth. Add sesame paste—the more you add, the richer it will be and the brighter its color—along with olive oil and toasted sesame oil. Chop pickled lemons into small pieces and add cooked chicken as is done in *mamzūj*. If you wish, you can sweeten it with sugar. Do not put in too much sumac because it will make the color drab. Garnish with pistachios, or, for a tastier and more fragrant dish, mix them in.

5.16 ***JŪDHĀBAT TABBĀLAH*** Boil chickens until half done. In a pan, moisten pure wheat bread crumbs with the chicken fat and broth, color with saffron, and tear up the chickens on top. If you want it sour, adjust with reconstituted pomegranate juice, lemon juice, sumac distillate, or sumac juice. Leave in a brick oven, either covered or uncovered. It comes out very nicely.

◆

5.17 **CHICKEN MEATBALLS** Make meatballs the size of hazelnuts from chicken breast and the meat of suckling lamb, seasoning them with the necessary spices. Then boil, fry in tail fat, and add honey, sugar, plenty of crushed boiled pistachios, mixed spices, saffron, and as much lemon juice as necessary. Add as much broth as needed and cook. Add a sprig of mint, spray with rose water, allow to settle, then remove and serve.

Section on Making Chicken Skin into Sausages in the Shape of the Chicken, with Chicken Meat and Other Stuffings—There Are Several Variations

5.18 **THE FIRST TYPE** Take a chicken and pluck it, but do not split its abdomen or craw. Put a little stick in its neck between the skin and the meat and use it to separate them from each other bit by bit. Blow strongly into the neck to separate the skin from the meat. Whenever you find something attached, keep blowing and pulling the skin away with the stick, then tie the skin tightly onto the leg bones with a linen thread. Split the chicken's back from the tail to the neck and separate the meat from the ribcage, leaving the leg and thigh bones as they are. Likewise, cut from inside the skin at the base of the wings, and remove the rib cage. Stuff the cavity with meat as you would a sausage casing, leaving the wings as they are, attached to the skin, to complete the appearance of a chicken. Sew the skin back the way it was and tie the neck tightly. Sew up the hindquarters also. Boil with sausages. You can bake it afterwards, or just serve it boiled.

THE SECOND TYPE You will need two chickens—the skin of one will be big enough to hold the meat of both. Boil the meat until done and pound it smooth in a mortar. Put it in a saucepan along with some chicken fat, a little sesame oil and olive oil, hot spices, and minced parsley, and fry brown with a little finely minced onion and mint. When done, stuff the chicken skin with the meat, tie up the neck, and put the breast bone back in to hold the chicken shape. Boil, fry, and put with other chickens cooked the usual way. It is impressive. 5.19

THE THIRD TYPE—STUFFED WITH AN EGG CAKE Inflate a chicken skin as described above. Insert a hook into its hindquarters and extract the intestines. Cut out everything inside with a knife and discard; if the intestines do not come out with a hook, cut them up into small pieces with a knife. Wash the chicken clean. Take eggs, break them in a vessel, and add hot spices, Chinese cinnamon, minced parsley, a little saffron, chicken fat, oil, and onions that have been fried until done. Pour into the hindquarters and sew shut. Then pour in by the neck until you are certain the whole body is filled, both skin and meat. Sew the head tightly shut, boil, and fry. This is an impressive dish. 5.20

THE FOURTH TYPE Instead of chicken, use ground red meat. All these variations are served on *tabbālah*s and square pasta along with stuffed pasta, garnishes, cold vegetable dishes, and *sanbūsak*. 5.21

5.22 Boil a chicken then fry it in sesame oil. Fry plenty of onions in sesame oil until half done, add minced parsley, mint, and rue, and bring to the boil. Add vinegar and a little chicken broth to cut the sharpness, then add hot spices, mixed spices, and enough saffron to give it a pleasing color. Add sugar and the chicken, and boil until thick. Add peeled pistachios and almonds.

5.23 **A variation with lemon juice** Add lemon juice along with the vinegar—more lemon juice than vinegar. In both these recipes, you can add pieces of quince, half-boiled separately, or leave out the quince; or you can add pieces of gourd. Add peeled pistachios and almonds. The foundation of this dish is properly thickening the sugar on a low fire.

5.24 **A variation, with sour grape juice** Boil the chicken and fry it. Fry minced dry onion with sesame oil, parsley, mint, rue, and hot spices. Add sour grape juice, sweeten with sugar, thicken on the fire, and add the chicken. This variation leaves out the nuts.

◈

5.25 **Chicken with a plain pistachio stuffing** Boil a chicken and fry in its own fat and sesame oil along with minced onion and coriander leaves until nearly browned and the onions are done. Add minced parsley and coriander leaves, hot spices, mixed spices, and a good amount of crushed toasted pistachios.

5.26 **A variation without pistachios called Egyptian *muʿarraq*** This contains crushed chickpeas instead and small meatballs flavored with hot spices. Serve on *kumāj* bread crumbs moistened with broth and chicken fat.

In the above dishes, you can add small meatballs made with spices, including coriander seeds and coriander leaves. They turn out very nicely.

MUKARDANAH Cut up pullets, each joint separately—the thigh in two pieces, and the wings and the back also separate—and boil. When done, pour on sesame oil to cover, then fry everything. Spray with rose water every so often, repeatedly until everything is browned. Sprinkle with coriander seeds, then remove and serve. 5.27

KĀMILIYYAH Boil chicken until half done and remove. To the broth add vinegar and good sugar, and thicken on the fire until the broth has the consistency of syrup. Then add the chicken along with saffron and thicken to a good consistency. Remove from the fire, transfer onto flatbread, and add blanched pistachios. Do not put mixed spices in this dish, or any spices except Ceylon cinnamon and mastic—those two are obligatory—and mint. All these dishes can be made with the chicken either cut up or whole, as desired, except for the bread-crumb stuffing dishes. 5.28

LEMON CHICKEN Cut chicken up, boil, and remove when done. Then take the broth and squeeze fresh lemons into it to make it sour. Add sugar, a sprig of mint, mastic, and Ceylon cinnamon. Add the chicken and bring to the boil two or three times. Then fry it and ladle out. 5.29

A VARIATION Boil chicken and thicken broth with peeled almonds pounded fine and strained into the broth through a piece of cloth. Add sugar and mint and boil until thick. Add pieces of gourd, and when thick, add fresh lemon juice until sour enough for individual taste. Bring to the boil and add mint. 5.30

5.31 **A SIMILAR VARIATION** Made with ground safflower seed instead of almonds. Cook until it has the consistency of the stew flavored with dried yogurt.

5.32 **ANOTHER VARIATION** Pound peeled blanched almonds to a paste. Cut up the chicken, boil, and fry in sesame oil. Add a sprig of mint, Ceylon cinnamon, and mastic. Put the pounded almonds in the chicken broth, and set on the fire with the chicken, without straining the solids from the almond milk. When done and thickened, add lemon juice, bring to the boil once, and ladle out. There is no sugar in this version. Those who dine late in the evening cook it without broth.

5.33 **ANOTHER VARIATION** Boil fattened chickens. When halfway done, peel almonds and pound until they swim in their own oil. Pour on them some of the chicken broth, strain through a good tight sieve, and return it to the chicken. Pour in 18 g to 21 g of cornstarch dissolved in chicken broth. Add sugar and cook until thick enough to be consumed with a soup spoon. When done, squeeze in strained fresh lemon juice until the mixture is sour enough for your taste. Bring to the boil two or three times and add peeled green pistachios, mint, Ceylon cinnamon, and mastic, and ladle it out. It is an exceptionally fine dish. And if you wish, add in large pieces of gourd.

5.34 **RECIPE FOR CHICKEN WITH POMEGRANATE JUICE** Pound pomegranate seeds fine, strain, and thicken the juice with ground almonds. Add sugar, mint, Ceylon cinnamon, and mastic, and thicken on the fire. Add a chicken that has been boiled and then fried and bring to the boil. If you want, add some gourd.

5.35 **A VARIATION** Boil dried pomegranate seeds.[15] Add sugar, mint, and Ceylon cinnamon. Add raw chicken washed clean, cook until done, and serve. This is the best version of the dish.

ANOTHER VARIATION Pound pomegranate seeds, strain the juice, sweeten with sugar, and thicken with ground almonds. Add enough ginger to make the mixture spicy, as well as pieces of quince and Fathi apples. Cut up a boiled chicken, fry, and add. This dish is called *rummān mukhaththar*. 5.36

ANOTHER VARIATION Strip seeds from fresh pomegranates, wash, dry, squeeze, and strain. Add sugar and a bunch of mint and put on the fire. Add fried chicken and cook until thick. Add pieces of gourd if you wish. 5.37

RECIPE FOR CHICKEN *KUZBARIYYAH* Boil a chicken and cut it up as described above. When done, fry with onions, sesame oil, hot spices, and garlic pounded with coriander leaves. After frying the chicken, pound coriander leaves smooth, put the broth on the chicken, and add the coriander, making a dish like *mulūkhiyyah*. 5.38

A BETTER VARIATION Cook the chicken as described and fry with garlic, minced onion, sesame oil, chicken fat, and hot spices. When done, pound coriander leaves smooth, strain thickly through a sieve several times with the chicken broth, and pour onto the chicken. Add a good handful of sieved pounded rice. It will thicken and develop a good flavor. This is a remarkable dish. 5.39

RECIPE WITH TAMARIND Boil and fry the chicken. Strain tamarind with the chicken broth after macerating it several times. Add sugar and thicken on the chicken on a low fire, as you would do with pomegranate. Add mint and spices. 5.40

RECIPE WITH BARBERRIES Boil barberries, strain, and thicken with sugar. Add boiled, fried chicken and add mint. 5.41

5.42 **RECIPE WITH RHUBARB** Boil rhubarb until it disintegrates and strain through a sieve. Add sugar, mint, and mixed spices, add chicken that has been boiled and fried, and bring to the boil.

5.43 **A VARIATION** Boil, fry, and then cut up a chicken. Fry onion and coriander leaves in sesame oil. Cut rhubarb into whatever pieces the cook prefers, add, and pour onto it a little broth.

5.44 **ANOTHER VARIATION** Boil rhubarb, strain through a sieve, and cook until done. Add mint, sweeten with a little sugar, bring to the boil, and add a fried chicken.

5.45 **RECIPE WITH QUINCE** Boil chicken, cut up, and fry in sesame oil with an onion. Split quinces, remove their seeds, and add to the chicken. Add broth and cook until the quinces are done. Pour on a little fresh lemon juice—just enough to make it sour—and a little sugar, saffron, mixed spices, mint, spices, and peeled pistachios. Let it settle and ladle it out.

5.46 **A VARIATION** Make the chicken with quinces as described, but substitute vinegar for the lemon juice, using more vinegar than lemon juice. Add peeled almonds and pistachios.

5.47 **ANOTHER VARIATION** Cook chicken as in the basic recipe, but this time fry the quinces and put them on the chicken. The quinces could also be fried in the other two recipes.

5.48 **ANOTHER VARIATION** Make it with chicken as described, and add quinces and Fathi apples, more apple than quince. Pour broth on it, as well as sugar, a little lemon juice, mixed spices, saffron, and nuts. Do not put too much lemon juice.

5.49 ***ZĪRABĀJ*** Boil and fry chicken. Take the chicken broth, add sugar, vinegar, and saffron, and thicken with peeled almonds which have been pounded and sieved and a little cornstarch. Add pistachios and almonds.

A VARIATION Put lemon juice with the vinegar; it comes out nicely. 5.50

*ANOTHER VERSION If you take sumac essence and add to the vinegar and lemon, it comes out nicely. 5.51

SUB-SECTION ON SUMAC ESSENCE It is made like sour grape essence. 5.52

VARIATION When you take sumac essence, extract sumac fruits with it, thicken with pounded almonds, add broth to break its sharpness, and sweeten with sugar. 5.53

CHICKEN WITH PARSLEY SAUCE Boil and fry chicken nicely. Take parsley, pick only its leaves, and pound smooth in an ordinary mortar or large marble mortar. Moisten the parsley with vinegar and pound until everything mixes with the vinegar. Beat so smooth that it can be picked up with bread. Add ginger, pepper, mixed spices, garlic, and mint and add the chicken while hot. It turns out well. 5.54

SOUR ORANGE CHICKEN Take sour orange or the sour part of citron, extract the pulp, and mix into syrup. Thicken to the consistency of beverage syrup. Fry the chicken and add. This is an unusual dish. When serving, plate the chicken and garnish with citron or orange flesh all over, on the breast and sides and underneath. 5.55

CHICKEN *KASHKĀT* Cook meat porridge with chicken in the clay oven. This is the best and most wonderful of dishes. 5.56

ANOTHER SOUR-ORANGE CHICKEN Boil chicken after cutting it up. Fry in sesame oil, chicken fat, and onions minced small until 5.57

the onions are done with the chicken as little browned as possible. Pound peeled almonds smooth until they swim in their oil. Extract them through a sieve with chicken broth to make a thickener. Add to the chicken, and bring to the boil several times. Peel the sour orange; the person who peels it should not be the one who squeezes it. Add to the broth along with the almonds and add a bit of mint leaf, Ceylon cinnamon, and mastic. Bring to the boil several times until it is sour enough for your taste, then ladle it out. You can sweeten it with sugar if you wish, but preparing it without is more correct.

5.58 **CAMPHOR-WHITE MEATBALLS** Take chicken breasts and slice thinly. Slice lean red meat, taking a *raṭl* of meat, by either Iraqi or Egyptian weight, for every breast. After washing it several times, pound everything finely with a cleaver to the consistency of peppercorns, so that it turns white and make it into meatballs. Melt tail fat as described above and fry the meat in it with 6 g of salt, 60 g of the cut-up white part of onions, grated Chinese cinnamon, and sieved pounded coriander seeds. Once it is fried, add the cooking water—use 300 g of hot water—and boil until it has reduced by half. Pound 90 g of peeled almonds or walnuts with rose water to the consistency of yogurt.[16] Add a handful of peeled chickpeas or pistachios and a bit of cloth containing pounded ginger and cumin, then wipe the sides of the pot. When the broth has been produced, remove from the fire if you want it plain. If you want it with eggs, beat almonds to a paste with rose water, mix with egg whites, put them on the dish, and garnish with the yolks. You could make this dish with delicate lamb alone.

Section on sweet chicken dishes

5.59 Take chicken, boil, and fry; it is sweetened in various ways.

5.60 **PISTACHIO CHICKEN** Blanch pistachios, dry in the open air, and pound in a mortar until they swim in their oil. Take a bowl of thick syrup, add the pistachios, and put on the fire. When it boils, add 18 g to 21 g of honey and 15 g of pounded, sieved cornstarch, and cook until thick enough that it will mound up if you put some of it on chicken breast. Add chard food coloring[17] which will be described in the appropriate place below, and leave the chicken in it to cook.

HAZELNUT CHICKEN The same, except that you toast hazelnuts, and peel and pound them. 5.61

ALMOND CHICKEN Peel almonds, pound, color well with saffron, and proceed as described. 5.62

POPPY-SEED CHICKEN Pound poppy seed and proceed as we have described. 5.63

THE QUEEN OF NUBIA Pound purslane seeds smooth and proceed with them as described. If you want the The Queen of Nubia to come out white, although people usually cook it black, pound the seeds so fine that they swim in their oil, then wash them in water several times—about ten—so that only the core remains. Strain the water from them in a cloth, and pound them in a mortar until they soften and become white and sticky. Then put them in the syrup, cook as described, and add the chicken. 5.64

LUBĀBIYYAH Sieve the crumbs of *kumāj* bread and color with saffron and rose water. Dry out and proceed as in the other sweet dishes. Add whole peeled pistachios. 5.65

ROSE-JAM CHICKEN Take rose preserve made with honey. Dissolve in syrup, add cornstarch, thicken, and add the chicken. 5.66

◆

CANDIED CHICKEN ON CROUTONS Take a chicken that has been boiled and then fried, and joint it. Cut crusts of *kumāj* bread into 5.67

pieces and fry in sesame oil. Make a very thick syrup with honey and put on the chicken. Put a little of the chicken broth on the fried bread to soften it and set the chicken on top, then pour the syrup over and allow to thicken on the chicken and bread. Add pistachios and a little sesame oil, and ladle and serve. This is a fine dish.

5.68 **A VARIATION** Sieve *kumāj* bread, color with saffron, and dry out. Then add sesame oil and syrup and cook on the fire until done. Cut up a sheet of the cornstarch confection called "horse hide," fry in sesame oil, and add to the bread crumbs. Add pistachios and a little sesame oil, and ladle it out. When done, add a cooked chicken. This is a delicious and unusual dish.

5.69 ***KHAWKHIYYAH*** Take fresh or dried cornelian cherry, which is *khawkh dubb*. Boil, strain the juice, and thicken with sugar. Moisten sieved bread crumbs with the cornelian cherry until bright red. Thicken and add to the chicken.

5.70 **JURJAN CHICKEN** Take sour jug yogurt and strain through a woolen wrapper. Dissolve white mustard in the sour yogurt, using enough to make distinctly hot. If it is not hot enough, add some finely pounded white mustard. Pound white sugar and add; mix in very well. Fry a chicken, put into the yogurt, and add fresh peeled pistachios. Mound the yogurt on the chicken and garnish with fresh pistachios and sour pomegranate seeds.

5.71 **CHICKEN WITH SYRIAN MULBERRIES** Macerate the mulberries and strain out the juice. Add sugar, thicken, and add mixed spices and mint. Put fried chicken in the mixture.

5.72 **VILLAGE-STYLE CHICKEN WITH SOUR CHERRIES** Boil ripe sour cherries with a little water. Strain and thicken on the fire with sugar. Add mint and a fried chicken.

CHICKEN WITH CORNELIAN CHERRIES Boil cornelian cherries, strain, and thick-en with sugar and mint. Add fried chicken and bring to the boil two or three times. 5.73

CHICKEN RICE Boil a fattened chicken. Cook rice pilaf as usual, substituting pistachios for chickpeas. When done, add rose water and two grains of musk and bring to the boil; it will become entirely flavored with musk. When done and ladled out, sprinkle with pounded sugar. The foundation of this dish is the fat. 5.74

SUB-SECTION ON HOW TO MAKE CHICKEN FAT[18] Cook fattened chickens in a pot and take two *ūqiyah*s of sheep-tail fat by Damascus weight (⅓ kg), as noted above, for every two chickens. Boil this in the pot with the chickens, then skim the fat. All of it will seem to be chicken fat; neither the appearance nor the taste of the tail fat will be noticeable. 5.75

RECIPE FOR CHICKEN CANAPÉS, KNOWN AS EGYPTIAN CANAPÉS 5.76
I describe them here only because there is chicken in them and this is the chapter on chicken. Obtain slack-dough bread containing borax from your baker. Split, cool, and clean out all the crumbs. Then return every loaf to its original shape and sieve the crumbs. Toast pistachios well but do not scorch, rub them so that they can be peeled, and crush in a mortar. Mince parsley, mint, and rue and squeeze fresh lemon juice on them. Boil chicken, and fry in olive oil. When done and cooled off, strip the meat from the bones and cut up crosswise with a knife until you have as much meat as crumbs. Do not rub with the grease. When done, take the crumbs, and rub with plenty of herbs, more than the crumbs; rub well. Pour the pistachios on top and drip with olive oil, a good deal of toasted sesame oil (enough to make it rich), and a little chicken fat. Add lemon juice and knead. When kneaded, add the chicken meat, taking care that it has not been rubbed with the grease. When the mixture is as sour

as you want, take olive oil, toasted sesame oil, and chicken fat, mix together, pour onto rose water, and beat. Moisten the loaves well with this mixture, inside and out, so that the bread absorbs it.

Put as much of the filling as you want inside: spread the loaf out, put the filling on the loaf, and reassemble it. Cut it with the knife into pieces as large as you want, then arrange them in pyramids with herbs on top. When violet, narcissus, and parsley are in season, arrange in the tray, first a layer of violet then a layer of herbs; it makes the canapés tasty. Do not leave them in the herbs overnight—the canapés will spoil. Garnish with an orange. If you want to perfume the filling with incense, take a Yemeni cup or a coconut shell and smoke it with ambergris. When it is full of smoke, put the filling in. Likewise, you can smoke the bread with ambergris when you moisten it. This is one of the most elegant of foods.

Chapter 6

Sautés and Related Dishes

First, sautés, kebabs, meatballs put on dishes to form part of garnishes, and so on. 6.1

Sanbūsak, for which there are four recipes

First recipe Take leg and loin meat, pound on a chopping block with a cleaver, and boil until done. Strain off the water and pound in a mortar until soft. Put in a brass pan and add melted tail fat along with coriander seeds, Chinese cinnamon, mastic, and pepper, and cook on the fire until it contracts. Then add two parts minced parsley, one part mint, and one-half part rue, and bring to the boil. Add lemon juice and vinegar and boil until they reduce, then stuff in *sanbūsak* wrappers in the usual way. This is the best kind. 6.2

Second recipe Add sumac, walnuts, and pistachios to the filling. 6.3

Third recipe Stuff *sanbūsak* wrappers with pieces of sweetmeat instead of meat, and fry. These make for a nice garnish. 6.4

Fourth recipe Color bread crumbs with saffron and add pounded sugar, honey, and sesame oil, following the recipe for *asyūṭiyyah* 6.5

pudding. When done, add poppy seeds and pistachios and stuff into the *sanbūsak* too.

Section on Egyptian kebabs

6.6 Cut the meat into thin kebabs and smoke them. Once smoked, moisten with water. Put sesame oil in a brass pan and fry the meat, repeatedly spraying with rose water and salt. When done and browned, sprinkle with coriander seeds, and they are ready to eat. Serve on dishes, either as a garnish or by itself.

6.7 **A variation** Cut filet and loin into thick kebabs and put them on a skewer. Rub with sesame oil, olive oil, pounded coriander seeds, and garlic. Roast on the skewer over a low fire.

6.8 **A delicious variation, the best there is** Cut filet into pieces, and cut tail fat into similar pieces. String on a skewer, alternating two pieces of meat with one piece of fat, and roast over a charcoal fire. Whenever the fat is about to drip, lift the end of the skewer so that the fat falls back on the meat, and rub it with rose water and sesame oil. Repeat until the meat is done. Sprinkle with coriander seeds, and it's ready to eat.

6.9 ***Another variation** Cut meat into thick kebabs, hang on a hook at the top of the clay oven until the blood and juices run, as you do with smoked kebabs, and put in a jug. Some people add apple and quince juices when they put the meat in the jug, and some add sugar, vinegar, mint, olive oil, rose hips, mastic, three sprigs of coriander, mixed spices, and Ceylon cinnamon. Seal the mouth of the jug and put it in a brick oven, without adding any water.

6.10 **Another variation** Cut meat into thick kebabs and put in a jug. Rub with olive oil and add hot spices, mixed spices, rose hips, mastic, and Ceylon cinnamon. Seal the jug and put it in a brick oven, without adding any water.

ANOTHER VARIATION Cut meat into kebabs, put on sheets of bread dough, and set in a brick oven. 6.11

ANOTHER VARIATION Put fat ribs on a roasting skewer, hang in the clay oven as with roast meat, then set a pudding of rice, milk, and saffron underneath. To me this is more delicious than plain roast meat. 6.12

ANOTHER VARIETY: FRANKISH ROAST Rub a fat lamb with salt, sesame oil, and rose water, and skewer on a long section of pole. Line charcoal the length of the lamb on the right and left sides, such that there is no fire directly under the lamb. Take your time roasting it and it will come out very nicely and cooked all the way through. Baste it over and over with sesame oil, rose water, and salt. 6.13

ANOTHER VARIETY, GEORGIAN KEBAB, WHICH I ONCE MADE FOR MY UNCLE AL-MALIK AL-ASHRAF, MAY GOD THE EXALTED SHOWER HIM WITH MERCY Pound loin meat smooth, add tail fat, onion, and coriander leaves, and sprinkle with pounded coriander seeds, pepper, Ceylon cinnamon, salt, and a drop of olive oil. Then take a sheet of caul fat, wash with hot water, open it out, and put the pounded meat on it. Roll the fat around it two or three times, folding the fat over from the ends, upper to lower and lower to upper. Whittle small skewers and use them to secure the fat onto the meat, then skewer and roast. This is one of the most delicious things you can eat. I have seen people half-boil the meat, mince it with an ordinary knife, and do as above. It tastes very good. 6.14

ANOTHER VARIATION Cut lamb liver into thick kebabs and boil them until done. Grease with a little olive oil, wrap with caul fat as for Georgian kebab, and roast as described. It is delicious. 6.15

6.16 **ANOTHER VARIATION** Take liver. Boil it, pound with the same amount of tail fat, add hot spices and mixed spices, and stuff sausages with it. It is delicious.

6.17 **A VARIATION WHICH IS A BEDOUIN SPECIALTY** Take fat lamb or kid, split lengthwise, and cut into pieces. Rub the pieces with saffron and hot spices such as pounded pepper, caraway, coriander seed, and Chinese cinnamon, and rub with a little olive oil to grease them. Then take pieces of rock or flagstones. Dig a small pit the size of the lamb, but deeper, and arrange the rocks in a nice layer. Build a large fire of wood or charcoal or whatever, using as much kindling as you can find. Make the fire hot enough to turn the stones red. Then take the burning coals out of the pit and remove the ashes with a rapid shaking motion, so that the stones do not cool off. When they are clean, make a lattice of tamarisk, willow sticks, or green cane, spread the meat out on it evenly, set it on the hot stones, and cover with the copper tray the Bedouins use—if you don't have one, with a large iron pan—and seal the edges with clay. Build a wood fire on the tray with the fuel equally distributed in all directions and leave until done. When done, remove the fire and take the meat out.

6.18 **ANOTHER VARIETY, THE MONK'S ROAST** Cut ribs, backbone, and loin, as large or small as you want. Close up the top of a pot with a cage or wide-mouthed strainer and pour in enough water to half fill it. But first put in onions, chickpeas, Ceylon cinnamon, mastic, and dill sprigs tied in a knot; cover with the lattice. Put the meat on the lattice, cover with a lid, seal the edges with stiff dough, and cook on low fire from evening to morning. When ready to eat, moisten *kumāj* bread crumbs with the broth and arrange the meat on them. Be sure no steam escapes from the pot.

◆

6.19 **FAUX MARROW** Make copper tubes shaped like thigh bones and seal one end. Boil liver until done. Use one part liver and one part tail fat; pound together until smooth. Stuff into copper tubes, seal the mouth with dough, put in boiling water, and boil until done. Shake out into a dish. It comes out the color and flavor of marrow.

Bread-crumb stuffing for roast meat

Take day-old *kumāj* bread crumbs and sieve. Mince parsley, mint, and rue very fine, and rub with the crumbs. Knead with lemon juice and sour grape juice, and add crushed toasted pistachios, hot spices, mixed spices, pepper, a little olive oil—not enough to taste—and toasted sesame oil. Knead everything together, smoke the lamb's body cavity, and stuff. 6.20

Second variety, with sumac Add sesame paste, sumac, and lemon juice. Soak sumac in the juice and strain; if there is too much sumac, it will come out dark and dull-colored. Add remaining ingredients—sesame paste and finely pounded walnuts—as described above for flavored stuffing. 6.21

Third variety, sweet This is like the bread-crumb stuffing for *sanbūsak* described above.[19] 6.22

Section on *mulūkhiyyah*, of which there are four types

Cut meat into small pieces. Pound coriander leaves, onions, and hot spices into the meat, and make into best-quality small meatballs, adding in Ceylon cinnamon and mastic too. Boil the remaining meat until half done and fry with a minced onion, garlic pounded with coriander leaves, and long pepper, coriander seed, salt, and caraway. Add tail fat and fry until the meat browns. Add the meatballs and fry until done. Add the meat broth and bring to the boil. Mince Jew's mallow fine, add, and boil—it should be neither too thin nor too thick and you should not be able to taste either salt or hot spices. 6.23

6.24 **SECOND TYPE OF *MULŪKHIYYAH*** Make the meat into small meatballs as usual. Take some more meat, pound fine, and boil. When done, strain, cook the meat until it contracts in tail fat, and add garlic pounded with coriander leaves, coriander seed, and hot spices. When browned and done, add the juice of fresh or pickled lemons, and bring to the boil several times to make it sour. Then return the broth to the meat and add finely minced Jew's mallow. Cook as usual;[20] it is quite tasty. There should be plenty of meat and spices and garlic, according to the disposition of the diner.

6.25 **THIRD TYPE, DRY *MULŪKHIYYAH*** Prepare the meat as usual for *mulūkhiyyah*, with garlic, spices, and coriander leaves. When done, have ready as much common mallow as needed, minced small and fine. Sprinkle with a handful of dried Jew's mallow rubbed by hand, mix together, and pour into the meat broth on the meat. Cook until the rubbed Jew's mallow is done; it comes out like fresh Jew's mallow. The proportion is a minced bunch of common mallow and a handful of dried Jew's mallow for every plate.

6.26 ***ANOTHER TYPE** Boil the meat as usual. Add the Jew's mallow and cook until done. Meanwhile, roast six onions until well done, then peel and pound smooth in a mortar with dry coriander, coriander leaves, garlic, and pepper. Add to the *mulūkhiyyah* when it is done. Pour melted tail fat on top and ladle out.

Section on Eggplant Dishes, of which there are eight types

6.27 **THE FIRST TYPE IS *BŪRĀNIYYAH***[21] Chop meat small, boil, and fry with onions, coriander leaves, and hot spices. Meanwhile, make meatballs with coriander leaves, onions, and hot spices, and fry with the meat. Take eggplants, gash with a knife, and put into salted water to draw out their black liquor, then squeeze out and fry along with dried onions in tail fat or sesame oil to cover. When the eggplants are browned and completely cooked, put them on the meat and sprinkle with coriander seeds and tail fat. Return six or seven ladles of broth to the pan, reduce the heat to low, and shake pan every so often until the broth evaporates. Ladle out and add coriander seeds, Chinese cinnamon, and pepper.

SECOND TYPE Boil eggplants till halfway done, and quarter lengthwise. Dry hard in the sun and set aside. When you cook eggplants out of season, soak them in water for two days and nights. Boil meat, and fry meatballs as for *kibrītiyyah* below. Boil the reconstituted eggplants separately until done and follow the procedure for *kibrītiyyah*. 6.28

A *BŪRĀNIYYAH* VARIATION This is made the same way as the first *būrāniyyah*. When done, dissolve dried yogurt in the meat broth with a little garlic, pour onto the *būrāniyyah*, and leave until done. It is good and delicious. 6.29

FOURTH TYPE, *KIBRĪTIYYAH* Take meat and chop small. Boil meatballs as for *būrāniyyah* and fry with pounded garlic, coriander seeds, coriander leaves, and tail fat. Add caraway, pepper, and Chinese cinnamon. When completely fried, cut eggplants in half and each half in four. Soak in salted water then wash off, put on the meat, and add a little meat broth. Pound *qirṭ* (table leeks), mince small, add, and leave on the dish. Keep boiling until the broth boils away and the eggplant is done, then ladle and serve. 6.30

FIFTH TYPE Make with meat, and flavor as usual, except for the eggplants—fry them as for *būrāniyyah*—and add the other ingredients. It comes out better that way. 6.31

SIXTH TYPE, STUFFED EGGPLANT Use large village eggplants. Cut from the calyxes, hollow out, and remove the core, but do not hollow out all the way to the skin; leave some thickness. Then take 6.32

meat, make into meatballs, and boil. When done, pound the meatballs again in a mortar until smooth. Put in a brass pan and add melted fresh tail fat, along with coriander seeds, caraway, pepper, Chinese cinnamon, and a lot of minced coriander and parsley leaves. Fry everything until it contracts. Flavor with salt and stuff the eggplants. Then replace the calyxes cut from the eggplants, securing with three skewers whittled from good wood. When done, put the eggplants in a brass pan and fry in tail fat until browned. Put in a dish and sprinkle with coriander seeds. When you ladle them out to serve, remove the skewers and discard.

6.33 **SEVENTH TYPE, *MADFŪNAH*** Fry meat and onions pounded with coriander leaves, as for *būrāniyyah*, and stuff eggplants as described above. Fry, put on the meat, and pour a little broth over them. Leave on a gentle fire until the broth dries away, then remove and serve.

6.34 **EIGHTH TYPE** Take meat, boil, and fry with meatballs as usual. When done, fry eggplants, and put on the meat. Then dissolve sesame paste with lemon juice and vinegar, add minced parsley and coriander leaves, hot spices, mint, and a stalk of rue. Sweeten with a little sugar—it should not be very sweet—and flavor it with garlic. Put on the meat and eggplants along with a little broth, bring to the boil three or four times, then remove and serve.

Section on the Ridged-Cucumber Dish, of which there are four varieties

6.35 **THE FIRST RECIPE** Cut meat in small pieces, boil them, and fry until browned. Quarter ridged cucumbers lengthwise. Stuff the cucumbers with coriander seeds, pepper, salt, and Chinese cinnamon, and arrange one on top of another so that their juice runs out. Put in a pot with sliced onions, coriander leaves, and pounded garlic. Add the meat and some of the cooking broth along with tail fat, and shake the pan lightly until the broth evaporates. If you want, add pounded walnuts and meatballs.

SECOND RECIPE After the dish is done, add dried yogurt mixed with broth, and bring to the boil several times. 6.36

THIRD RECIPE This is similar to the first recipe, except that after you split the ridged cucumbers, you hollow out the large ones and stuff them with meat that has been half-boiled and pounded smooth. Do not leave them whole or they will not absorb the broth and fat, a lot of water will come out when you eat them, and they will be tough. 6.37

FOURTH RECIPE After peeling the cucumbers, split in four without separating the pieces. Boil, place in a strainer so the juice can run, and fry brown in sesame oil. Cut meat small, boil together with meatballs, and fry separately from the ridged cucumbers. Chop onions small and fry with a little broth and sesame oil or tail fat. Put the meat on them with a little broth and bring to the boil several times. Put the fried ridged cucumbers on top along with some broth and fat and bring to the boil. Then add some minced parsley, vinegar, and spices, bring to the boil several times, and remove and serve. 6.38

***FIFTH RECIPE** Boil the meat as described above. Take ridged cucumbers, cut out circles in them, and stuff with pounded meat. Put meat on other ridged cucumbers that have been quartered lengthwise but not stuffed, and put the stuffed cucumbers on top. Add broth and tail fat, sauté carefully until done, and sprinkle with coriander. Do not use whole ridged cucumbers; they will become flabby. 6.39

Section on taro dishes, for which there are five recipes

6.40 **THE FIRST RECIPE IS *MUTAWAKKILIYYAH*** Boil meat. Make meatballs as usual and fry in fat. Chop onions and fry with the meat. Add pounded garlic with a good bit of coriander leaf, hot spices, and coriander seeds, and fry until done. Cut taros in half and boil until froth rises. When it does, strain off the water, pour on a little salt and a drop of olive oil, and rub well—wash several times until you have cleaned off the stickiness. Then put them on the meat and cover in meat broth. Chop spinach, pound smooth with coriander leaves, and add. Boil on low fire until well done and little broth is left. Let settle, then ladle and serve.

6.41 **SECOND RECIPE, *SITT AL-SHUNAʿ*** Boil meat, add meatballs as usual, and fry in fat along with pounded garlic and coriander leaves, coriander seeds, pepper, and Ceylon cinnamon. Also cut up onions for it, and fry together. When done, take boiled taros and wash as described for *mutawakkiliyyah*. When they are clean, fry in sesame oil on a low fire until browned. When brown, lay on the meat and add a little broth—an amount that will evaporate quickly—and boil on the fire until only fat remains. Sprinkle with toasted pistachios, coriander seeds, and hazelnuts, then ladle and serve.

6.42 **THIRD RECIPE** Make with everything described for *sitt al-shunaʿ* and along with the broth, add sesame paste, finely pounded toasted hazelnuts, and minced parsley and coriander leaves. Bring to the boil three times, ladle, and serve.

6.43 **FOURTH RECIPE** Made the usual way, as with *sitt al-shunaʿ*, but along with the meat broth, add sesame paste, vinegar, a little lemon juice, sugar, parsley, coriander leaves, and saffron. Bring to the boil several times, then remove and serve.

FIFTH RECIPE Boil meat. Prepare meatballs and fry them in tail fat with onions and coriander seeds. When done, prepare taro as for *sitt al-shunaʿ* and add to meatballs. Boil a strong syrup, adding a little honey, but not enough to give a sharp taste. Pour the syrup on the meat and taro and thicken well. Add toasted peeled pistachios, poppy seeds, and a little saffron. Ladle and serve. This is a tasty dish. 6.44

Section on cauliflower, for which there are three recipes

THE FIRST RECIPE Boil meat with chickpeas. Prepare meatballs as for the taro dishes and fry with onions, pounded garlic, and coriander leaves. When done, boil cauliflower until done and cut each head into five or six sections. Add to the pot with the meat, add broth to cover, and add in the boiled chickpeas. There should be a lot of coriander leaf mixed with table leeks. Put on low fire until the water evaporates, break eggs on top, cover until the eggs are done, ladle out, and serve. 6.45

SECOND RECIPE Make as in the first recipe. Boil the cauliflower, fry in tail fat until done and browned, and add the meat. Then take dried yogurt, dissolve in meat broth, add to the meat, and leave until it comes to the boil two or three times. Ladle out and serve. This is a particularly tasty dish. 6.46

THIRD RECIPE This is made like *sitt al-shunaʿ*. Also add North African soy sauce mixed with vinegar and lemon juice. 6.47

Section on spinach: four recipes

THE FIRST RECIPE Chop meat and boil with chickpeas and an onion until done. Prepare meatballs and fry the meat and meatballs in fat with coriander leaves and an onion. When browned, add the chickpeas. Clean spinach, cut leaves in half, and add to the meat. 6.48

Cover the pot and leave until quite done. Sprinkle with coriander seeds, break eggs on top, and leave until ready.

6.49 **SECOND RECIPE** Cut meat in big pieces and boil with chickpeas. When done, remove the meat, fry in fat or olive oil, and pour the broth on it. Wash rice, add, and cook until done. Put in a large quantity of whole garlic cloves. Separately, boil whole spinach leaves until done, then add to the rice and leave to cook until dry and firm. There should be plenty of fat in it.

6.50 **THIRD RECIPE** Similarly made, with peeled heads of garlic and chickpeas, but the rice should be soupy so it can be consumed with a soup spoon, and with the spinach swimming in it.

6.51 **FOURTH RECIPE** Noodles instead of rice with the spinach. Break eggs on top.

◆

6.52 ***RABĪʿIYYAH*, A WELL-KNOWN DISH** There should be plenty of thyme and broth in it. An unusual version uses fresh pistachios in place of the usual fava beans. It should be fried in fat until done with garlic, coriander leaves, onions, and hot spices. Add peeled green pistachios and fry until done with plenty of fat. If you want, break eggs on top. If the pistachios are dry, the dish will be green.

Kuzbariyyah, of which there are two types

6.53 **THE FIRST TYPE** Boil meat, and prepare meatballs. Trim coriander leaves from their stalks and pound smooth. Fry the meat and meatballs with garlic, coriander leaves, and hot spices. Pour the meat broth and the pounded coriander leaves over the meat so that the dish becomes like *mulūkhiyyah.*

SECOND TYPE Cook the *kuzbariyyah* as described in the chicken chapter, thickened with pounded almonds. This is the best coriander dish. 6.54

Section on the garlic dish, of which there are two types

THE FIRST TYPE Take meat and boil it, and make meatballs. Pound garlic well with coriander leaves and add hot spices and coriander seeds. Fry the garlic and the meat with fat and plenty of onion, spraying with broth over and over as it fries, then ladle out. 6.55

THE SECOND TYPE, WHICH IS THE BEST THERE IS Boil meat as described above. Then take large heads of garlic, peel the cloves, leaving them whole, and put them on the meat. Return a large amount of the cooking liquid and boil on a low fire until the garlic is done and the broth has boiled away, leaving only the fat. Be sure to use a generous quantity of coriander leaves. The fat has an especially good flavor. 6.56

Section on rhubarb, for which there are two recipes

The first is like the two rhubarb recipes in the chicken chapter, substituting red meat and meatballs for the chicken. In the fried version, you add crushed chickpeas. 6.57

For the second recipe,[22] the meat should be in large chunks and the meatballs also large, made with rice and crushed chickpeas. Add chard stalks as well. 6.58

Section on *Narjisiyyah*, of which there are three varieties

6.59 **THE FIRST VARIETY** Take meat, chop small, and boil with chickpeas. Pound meat as usual, adding rice and crushed chickpeas, and make into small meatballs. Fry the meat and the meatballs with onions and hot spices until browned. Then wash rice; mince coriander leaves; pound coriander seeds, pepper, and Ceylon cinnamon; and add to the meat. Add broth to cover, along with chickpeas, peeled whole garlic cloves, and peeled carrots slivered as thin as necessary. Put on a low fire until the rice is done; there should be plenty of fat on it. When done, break whole eggs over the dish, making a lattice of the whites mixed with spices and coriander leaves, and putting the yolks on top.

6.60 **SECOND VARIETY** This is the usual *narjisiyyah*, but when it is done, pour in dried yogurt dissolved with fresh lemon juice and a little broth. Let it cook down on a low fire. Top with eggs as usual.

6.61 **THIRD VARIETY** The usual *narjisiyyah*, but if you have *ṣarkhadī* cheese, sliver it like the carrots and add. Make a layer of meat, rice, and carrots, and a layer of the cheese, and arrange in a pan. Cook on a low fire with broth and plenty of fat. Then add spices and coriander leaves to egg whites, put them on the pan, set the unbroken yolks on top, remove, and serve.

Recipe for *Dīnāriyyah*

6.62 **FIRST RECIPE** Boil meat with crushed chickpeas. Make meatballs with rice, crushed chickpeas, and spices in them as is done in making such dishes. Fry everything in fat with coriander leaves pounded with spices and a little garlic. Add a little of the broth and some carrots cut into thin dinar coin shapes, cook on a low fire until done, and ladle out. Throw in boiled chickpeas while frying and break eggs on top.

SECOND RECIPE Make like the *dīnāriyyah* above, substituting vinegar with honey or sugar for the broth. If you wish, make it with fruit molasses instead of honey, with a little broth to reduce the sharpness. Once thickened and done, ladle out and serve. 6.63

THIRD RECIPE Cut meat small and boil. Make small meatballs flavored with spices and coriander leaves, and fry everything in tail fat. Sliver peeled carrots thinly as for *narjisiyyah*, put them on the meat, and cover.[23] Do not put the carrots in the water but leave to cook in the fat on a low fire until done and exuding carrot juice. 6.64

SECTION ON ONION DISHES, FOR WHICH THERE ARE THREE RECIPES

THE FIRST IS AN ONION DISH WHICH IS BETTER THAN MANY OTHERS—BETTER EVEN THAN SWEETMEAT Peel dried onions, wash, and boil till falling apart. Mix together, let cool, and squeeze out the cooking liquid. Chop, boil, and fry meat. Make plain meatballs as for the taro dish above and fry with the meat until they brown and contract. Add vinegar and honey, or sugar if you prefer, to the onions, and cook on low fire. Add saffron, mixed spices, and tail fat to cover and thicken on a low fire. Then add the meat and bring to the boil twice for the flavor of the mixture to enter the meat. Thicken on a low fire until it has the consistency of *khābiṣah* pudding.[24] It can be made sweet or sour, according to the diner's preference. Add fresh mint and ladle the meat out. Then thicken the onions like a sweetmeat, remove, and serve. 6.65

SECOND RECIPE Cut meat up and boil with crushed chickpeas. Make spiced meatballs with rice and crushed chickpeas and fry in 6.66

fat. Peel onions, split in half, and fry in fat with the meat and meatballs. When nearly done, add some of the broth with vinegar, honey, mixed spices, saffron, and sprigs of mint. Ladle and serve.

6.67 **THIRD RECIPE** Boil meat, make meatballs, and fry everything. Peel small onions and add to the meat while frying. When half done, return the broth to the meat with spices and plenty of coriander leaves added in. Boil until broth evaporates, only fat is left, and onions are done.

Section on cabbage dishes, for which there are two recipes

6.68 **THE FIRST RECIPE** Cut meat in large pieces, boil, and fry. Return the liquid to the meat and boil chickpeas in it. Chop cabbage small, and boil separately; after washing everything, put with rice, add meat broth, and cook until completely done. Add in whole garlic cloves.

6.69 **SECOND RECIPE** Cut meat up and boil. Make meatballs as for the taro dish above. Fry everything in fat along with garlic pounded with coriander leaves, hot spices, and coriander seeds; make sure to use plenty of coriander leaves. When the meat has fried brown, return broth to it and add shredded cabbage and tail fat. Cook until the cabbage is done, the broth has evaporated, and only the fat is left. This is a tasty dish.

Section on sour-grape dishes, for which there are five recipes

6.70 **THE FIRST RECIPE** Strip sour grapes from the stalks, and boil till they fall apart. Strain away the juice and transfer onto the fire. Boil pieces of raw meat and large meatballs—make sure these are made with crushed chickpeas and rice. Boil with chard stalks, onions, and mint, and float in it pieces of gourd, eggplants quartered lengthwise, and sour apples split in half with seeds and cores removed. Add fresh thyme, or dried if fresh is unavailable. Adding purslane is good too. Thicken with bread, or better yet, pounded rice, because it will then come out white.

To thicken with bread, boil bread with the sour grapes and strain. To thicken with rice, pound rice and put in. Add the thickener when the meat is done, and put in garlic pounded with coriander leaves and hot spices.

SECOND RECIPE Chop meat, boil, and fry. Make meatballs with 6.71
rice and chickpeas as usual for fried dishes then fry with onions, hot spices, and coriander leaves. Next, strip sour grapes from their stalks, crush in a dish with a stone, and strain the juice. When it is clear, add to the meat, put in a sprig of mint, bring to the boil several times, then remove and serve.

THIRD RECIPE Strip the sour grapes and dry in the sun. When 6.72
you want to cook with them, boil, strain the juice, and thicken with pounded rice and sour yogurt so that it takes on the color of a sour grape-dish made with fresh grapes. Add vegetables according to the season, such as chard, carrots, garlic, onions, and turnips, and color the stew green with chard food coloring.

Making the chard food coloring: Pound chard leaves, strain off the liquid, and boil the residue on the fire. It will separate—when it does, leave a while and strain the water from it. The green part will remain in the bottom of the pan. Beat well and use to color whatever you want.

This needs a skillful cook in order for it to acquire the color of a sour-grape dish made with fresh grapes.

6.73 **FOURTH RECIPE, A FAUX SOUR-GRAPE DISH** Boil meat and fry in fat. Make meatballs as for the sour-grape dish and add meat broth and seasonal vegetables. When done, add sour yogurt and lemon juice to the broth. Thicken with rice flour and color green with chard as described above. Cook with garlic in the usual way for a sour-grape dish, taking care not to put in too much yogurt. It comes out like the sour-grape dish in color and flavor when cooked well by someone skilled in matching its color and flavor. Other cold vegetable dishes will be described in their proper place.

6.74 **FIFTH RECIPE, CALLED THE BEGINNING AND THE END** Boil sour grapes until thick then strain. Pound light-colored raisins smooth and pour the sour grape juice on them. Knead and strain a second time, and cook with meat and vegetables as is usually done for sour-grape dishes.

Section on turnip dishes, of which there are three types

6.75 **THE FIRST TYPE** Chop meat and boil with chickpeas. Make meatballs as usual for fried dishes and fry with tail fat, garlic pounded with coriander leaves, hot spices, and coriander seeds. When brown, add peeled turnips cut in medium pieces, neither too small nor too large, and cover the pot. The turnips will release water. Uncover repeatedly until they are done in the liquid they exude, then break eggs over the dish. This variation has lots of coriander leaves in it. Remember to also put in chickpeas and fry with a lot of chopped onions.

6.76 **SECOND TYPE** Color the turnips with saffron and cook the same way.

6.77 **THIRD TYPE** Make using half turnips and half carrots. This is called *mashriqiy-yah*. It comes out very nicely.

Section on green almonds, for which there are two recipes

THE FIRST RECIPE Chop meat small and boil. Make meatballs and fry in fat with coriander leaves, pounded hot spices, and onions. Cut "eagle" almonds in half. Partly peel, boil until done, and add to the meat. Return a little of the broth, make sour with a little lemon juice, and cook until done. Add garlic if you wish. 6.78

THE SECOND RECIPE Boil the green almonds until they fall apart. Macerate and strain. Add meat as for the sour-grape juice dish and thicken with pounded rice. Add a little yogurt and some lemon juice to make it sour, as in the sour-grape juice dish. Then boil halved almonds until done and add so that it has the appearance of the first almond dish. 6.79

Section on sumac, for which there are five recipes

THE FIRST RECIPE Take sumac, pound it, shake the fruits, and take out the seeds. Soak the fruits in water. Mince parsley, mint, and rue, sieve bread crumbs, and knead them with the herbs until they wilt. Add the sumac along with hot spices, dried thyme—use plenty of thyme—and mixed spices. Knead with lemon juice, sesame paste, a little yogurt, and pounded toasted walnuts to make a stuffing. Cut small pieces of pickled lemon into it. Then take the water in which you soaked the sumac and add to the pot. Put in meat and meatballs—kneading some minced lemon into the meatballs—and boil; make the meatballs big, with rice and chickpeas kneaded into them. Add chard stalks, eggplant, gourd, pieces of quince, carrots when in season, and turnips. When everything is done, put in minced *qirṭ* (table leeks) and garlic pounded with coriander leaves. Add the stuffing, with crushed chickpeas in it, to the meat broth and bring to 6.80

the boil exactly twice. Make it as sour as you wish. Do not let it boil too much or put too much sumac or it will turn black. If you want to make it even more sour, extract the sumac berries with lemon juice and likewise with meat broth to avoid darkening the color. Then ladle and serve.

6.81 **THE SECOND RECIPE** Make as described above, but add boiled pounded meat, then pound it again and fry in fat until it contracts. Then add sumac and vegetables. This is a nice dish.

6.82 **THE THIRD RECIPE, *MADFŪNAH*** Make it like the sumac dish, but put in eggplant, stuffed as described earlier,[25] and the same vegetables.

6.83 **THE FOURTH RECIPE, *FĀKHITIYYAH*** This is made like the sumac dish, but with plenty of yogurt to give it the color of a wood dove's plumage.

You can put sesame paste, almonds, and walnuts in all these dishes, or hazelnuts, which are better and more wholesome.

6.84 **THE FIFTH RECIPE** Pound sumac, soak in water, and strain. Put in a pot, sweeten with sugar, thicken with pounded peeled almonds extracted with sumac juice, and cook down on the fire. Boil meat, fry in fat with onions, and add to the sumac. Boil until the meat tastes sour, then bring out the flavor with lemon juice.

6.85 ***THE SIXTH RECIPE** Boil fat meat with Chinese cinnamon, mastic, and sesame oil in two times enough water to cover. Add meatballs made with spices and *qirṭ* (table leeks), rice and mint. When done, remove the broth. Put the meat in tail fat and return a little of the broth. Boil sumac with a piece of bread so that none of its flavor gushes,[26] and 3 g of salt. Add the juice to the meatballs. Arrange eggplants fried in sesame oil or tail fat in the pot. If the eggplants are stuffed with meat and spices like *sanbūsak* and then fried, so much the better. Then put in all the spices, mixed spices, mint, sesame paste, almonds, walnuts, and pounded garlic, and let settle on the fire. Remove and serve. It turns out marvelously.

Section on cowpeas, for which there are two recipes

THE FIRST RECIPE Cook meat as for the fried-garlic dish. Cut off the tops, tails, and withered parts of fresh cowpea pods. Take out the peas, add to the meat, and return a little of the meat broth. Leave on low fire until cowpeas are done, broth has evaporated, and only fat and spices remain. 6.86

THE SECOND RECIPE Cook the same way, but with cowpeas alone. The key to this dish is using plenty of coriander leaf. 6.87

◆

CROCUS BULBS These are cooked like *kuzbariyyah*. Peel crocus bulbs, add to the meat with a little broth and a good deal of fat on a low fire. When done, ladle and serve. 6.88

Section on rice dishes—nine recipes

THE FIRST DISH IS *MUHALLABIYYAH* Boil meat. Pick over rice, wash, color with saffron, add to the meat, and boil until done. For more color, increase the amount of saffron. Pour honey or pounded sugar and tail fat on it and leave on low fire until the rice grains cook up separately. Ladle out and sprinkle with sugar. Syrup strengthened with honey can also be used. Sprinkle also with pistachios. 6.89

SECOND DISH, WHITE RICE *BARDAWĪLĪ* Cook the same way, but include soaked whole chickpeas and omit the saffron and honey. 6.90

6.91 **THIRD DISH, *RUKHĀMIYYAH*** Boil meat in a little water until done, then set the meat aside. Pour into the broth three times as much milk. Bring to the boil and put in washed, picked-over rice and some tail fat. When done and the rice grains have cooked up separately, add the meat, refined white sugar, and plenty of fat. Ladle out.

6.92 **FOURTH DISH, RICE PILAF** Boil meat with soaked whole chickpeas, fry in tail fat, and return the broth to it. Add washed, picked-over rice and leave on the fire until done. Strain out excess water, pour in melted tail fat, cover the pot, and leave a while. Instead of chickpeas, you can use peeled green pistachios. Sprinkle with sugar and spray with rose water; ladle out and serve.

6.93 **FIFTH VARIATION, YELLOW PILAF** Color the rice with saffron and make in the usual way, but add 4½ g of ground camphor for every *raṭl* of rice, Hama weight (2 kg).

6.94 **SIXTH DISH, WHITE-GRAIN YELLOW-GRAIN PILAF** Take meat, boil, and fry as usual for pilaf. Then boil white rice separately and color the rice yellow with saffron; boil and strain the water. Put the yellow rice on the meat, add tail fat, and cook a while. Then put the white rice on it and leave to cook a while. Instead of chickpeas, you can use peeled fresh pistachios. Ladle and serve.

6.95 **SEVENTH DISH, RICE WITH CORNELIAN CHERRIES** This is made like *fāʾiziyyah* below but comes out better and far nicer.

6.96 **EIGHTH DISH, *FĀʾIZIYYAH*** Take meat, boil, and cook until done. Take pomegranate seeds, pound, and strain thickly. Put rice in meat broth—use only a little broth—and cook the rice until done. Moisten with the strained pomegranate by spoonfuls and sweeten with honey or sugar, according to disposition. Pound stalks of mint with the pomegranate. Cook the rice on a low fire with tail fat until done and thickened enough that it can be ladled out on the serving dish in mounds.

Ladle and serve all rice dishes the same way.

NINTH DISH, SERVANTS' *KASHKIYYAH* Boil meat. Make meatballs containing rice and crushed chickpeas, and boil. Boil soaked whole chickpeas with the meat, and boil washed, picked-over rice in the broth until done. Then moisten with sour yogurt and a little lemon juice. Add minced parsley and table leeks, pickled lemons cut in small pieces, and tail fat, and leave until done. Ladle and serve. 6.97

***TENTH DISH—MAKING *KHĀTŪNĪ* RICE, WHICH IS WONDERFUL** 6.98
Boil water and add tail fat and chicken fat, both melted without salt. Add rice, and when half-done, let the water reduce till nothing is left but the fat. Take pistachios toasted in sesame oil, crush, and add pounded sugar. Put them in the rice—put plenty—spray with rose water and a little musk, and serve. It is outstanding.

Section on *al-Qamḥiyyah* (whole-wheat dish), of which there are two types

THE FIRST TYPE I will not describe it,[27] as it is so well known. 6.99

THE SECOND TYPE Cook wheat and moisten with tepid milk instead of cold water. Leave on the fire until it thickens. (The wheat should first be half-boiled and washed in cold water several times, then returned to cook as usual.) 6.100

Kashk (crushed-wheat dish), of which there are two types

THE FIRST TYPE It is too well known to describe.[28] 6.101

6.102 **SECOND TYPE** After straining it, add dried yogurt mixed with fresh lemon juice and whole chickpeas. Eggplants, turnips, carrots, chard stalks, and gourd can go in too.

Section on vinegar dishes, for which there are several types

6.103 **THE FIRST TYPE IS *ḤUBAYSHIYYAH*** Take black raisins, remove the seeds, and pound smooth, spraying them with vinegar as you do, and strain them with sharp vinegar. Boil meat until half done and add the raisins and vinegar and a little broth. Make meatballs with rice and crushed chickpeas in them, and add. Boil chard ribs, peeled whole onions, carrots if in season—cutting them in half lengthwise—and cut-up gourds if in season. Sweeten with a little honey, fruit molasses, or sugar, add mint and mixed spices, and cook down to taste, though thick is better than thin. Remove and serve.

SECOND TYPE, *ZĪRABĀJ*, OF WHICH THERE ARE TWO VARIETIES

6.104 **THE FIRST VARIETY** Take meat, boil until done, and add crushed chickpeas. When the chickpeas are done, add vinegar, honey or sugar, saffron, pieces of quince and Hadithi apples, and—if you want—peeled almonds, jujubes, and pistachios as well, and fresh mint. Thicken on the fire and ladle it out.

6.105 **THE SECOND VARIETY** This is made the same way, but with the addition of starch to thicken it. Color it yellow.

THIRD TYPE, THICKENED VINEGAR DISH, OF WHICH THERE ARE TWO VARIETIES

6.106 **THE FIRST VARIETY** Boil meat, make the sort of meatballs used in fried dishes, and fry them brown in tail fat. Add minced onions as well, having already fried them in fat. When done, add parsley, mint, and sprigs of rue, then pour in vinegar, sesame paste, mixed spices, toasted hazelnuts or pounded pistachios, and a little garlic. Bring to the boil several times so that it thickens, and ladle and serve.

THE SECOND VARIETY Similarly made, but instead of the usual fried meat, make it with meat that has been pounded and cooked until it contracts. It is made as above with sesame paste, vinegar, herbs, and hazelnuts. 6.107

FOURTH TYPE, *MAṢŪṢ*, MADE LIKE CHICKEN *MAṢŪṢ*[29] 6.108

*FIFTH TYPE, SWEETENED *SIKBĀJ* Uses meat, gourd, pepper, Ceylon cinnamon, onions, saffron, and wine vinegar. Put the meat in the pot, add water to cover, and cook until the water boils away. Then add pounded Ceylon cinnamon, pepper, olive oil, and one onion, and fry well. When it smells good, add hot water—just a little, as the gourd will release some water. When the water boils, add the gourd, cut into pieces, and when it returns to the boil, add chopped onions. When it smells good, sprinkle with salt before putting in the vinegar, so that it is not cut;[30] add salt to taste. Instead of gourd, you can use fried taro or "female" taro.[31] Before putting in the vinegar, add raisins, jujubes, blanched almonds, and sugar, then the vinegar. Having already put in saffron, now add mixed spices, using the following blend: equal quantities of wine vinegar and honey or sugar, plus saffron and almonds—blanched, peeled, and split in half—along with ambergris and all the mixed spices, and cook to the right consistency. Ladling them into bowls improves them. 6.109

Two variations on sour-orange stew

THE FIRST RECIPE Boil meat. Make meatballs and fry them brown with onions, coriander leaves, and spices. Sliver carrots as for *narjisiyyah* and chop up chard ribs and onions into pieces of the same small size. Put them on the meat with a little broth, and when 6.110

done, squeeze in sour oranges along with mint, mixed spices, and crushed chickpeas.

How to squeeze sour oranges: Peel off a ring from the middle of the orange three finger-widths wide before squeezing, so that none of the flavor of the peel gets into the juice.

6.111 **THE SECOND RECIPE** Cook sour-orange stew as usual. Take meatballs the size of an orange and put them in the broth. When they are done, take egg yolks by themselves and add a little finely ground chickpea flour and enough saffron to color them orange. Put the meatballs in the yolks to coat them and make them look like oranges. Add to the broth and boil so that the egg hardens on the meatballs. Take the egg whites and some whole eggs with their yolks. Pound hot spices, rue, parsley, mint, and coriander leaves and beat them with the eggs. Put on the sour-orange stew in the pot and boil it until the eggs are cooked. Put this egg white netting on the dish and set the meatballs colored orange with egg yolk on top, as if they were a garnish of oranges. Do not put too much chickpea flour in the yolks, just enough to make them stick on the meatballs.

Section on lemon-juice stew, of which there are three main recipes[32]

THE FIRST, DONE TWO WAYS

6.112 ***FUQQĀʿIYYAH*** Take meat, chop up, and boil. Make small meatballs, using crushed chickpeas and rice. Fry the boiled meat in tail fat with onions, coriander leaves, hot spices, and the crushed chickpeas boiled with the meat. When browned, return some of the broth. Cut small chard ribs in half and add to the stew until done. Take good quality lemon juice and pour on the stew, adding some broth to cut its sharpness. Take eggs, beat the whites with minced parsley, mint, and rue, along with both hot and mixed spices, and add to the pot. Put the yolks on the whites after they have stiffened ever so slightly. Ladle the stew out. Arrange the whites on the stew in the serving dish as a lattice and sprinkle with Chinese cinnamon.

The other way is *fuqqāʿiyyah* without the egg lattice. 6.113

THE SECOND VARIATION, THE SAFFLOWER DISH, OF WHICH THERE ARE TWO KINDS

THE FIRST KIND Boil and fry meat. Pound safflower with salt 6.114
and a little rice or wheat so that it does not become bitter. Strain with meat broth. Add some water, strain two or three times more, and add to the meat. Put in chard and large meatballs and thicken on the fire. When done, add lemon juice and bring to the boil several times. Put in a sprig of mint and bring to the boil, then remove and serve.

THE SECOND KIND is made like the regular safflower dish but 6.115
with the addition of white sugar and carrots in season. If you wish, use gourd and chard.

THE THIRD VARIATION Make meat into meatballs following the 6.116
usual recipe. Take peeled, finely pounded almonds and milk them into the meat broth. Return the broth to the meat and boil with sugar until it thickens. Then add lemon juice and sprigs of mint, bring to the boil two or three times, thicken with a little cornstarch, and ladle out.

Section on quince stew, of which there are two types

THE FIRST TYPE Boil meat. Make small meatballs, fry in tail 6.117
fat with onions and coriander leaves, and add a little of the broth. Quarter quinces and remove seeds and core. Put the quinces on the

meat with a little saffron, mixed spices, and some honey or sugar, and leave until the meat is halfway done. Add some lemon juice and coriander leaves and boil until the quinces are done. Add peeled pistachios, ladle and serve.

6.118 **THE SECOND TYPE** This is made like quince stew, but using vinegar instead of lemon juice. Fry the quinces in sesame oil and put them in as usual.

Section on apple dishes

6.119 **THE FIRST RECIPE** Boil sour apples, drain, and add to meat and meatballs which have been fried with onions and coriander leaves. If the flavor needs improving, sour with lemon juice, but not so much that it can be tasted. Put in mint and add boiled apples cut in half along with chard ribs. Thicken with sour yogurt as desired.

6.120 **THE SECOND RECIPE** Fry boiled meat and meatballs in the usual way with onions and coriander leaves. Cut apples in half, pick out the seeds and cores, and put the apples on the meat along with plenty of fat. Shake three or four times so that the apples absorb the fat. Add the meat broth and boil until apples are done and some of the broth has evaporated. Make sour with lemon juice and ladle out.

6.121 **THE THIRD RECIPE** Chop meat up, boil, and fry. Add Fathi or Hadithi apples—the Fathi are best—after removing seeds and cores. Add meat broth, sugar, a little saffron, mixed spices, and peeled pistachios. Set on a low fire until sugar thickens and apples are done.

6.122 **THE FOURTH RECIPE** Similarly made, but with the addition of freshly squeezed lemon juice, vinegar, or sour grape juice, according to the mixture desired.

Section on fresh fennel stew, two types

THE FIRST TYPE Boil meat and fry with coriander leaves, onions, hot spices, and a little garlic. Then choose fennel stalks, cut in half, and put on the meat. Add a little of the broth and some tail fat, and boil until done. When the broth has boiled away, remove and serve. 6.123

SECOND TYPE Add sweetened vinegar along with the broth that has been put on the meat. Otherwise, make the same way as the first type. 6.124

Section on lentil dishes, for which there are four recipes

THE FIRST RECIPE is of two kinds. Market folk and the bulk of people cook the first kind[33]—so there is no point in giving a recipe here. It is worth noting, though, that adding carrots, chard, large taros, and saffron will improve it. 6.125

SECOND RECIPE Boil lentils until done. Pound meat, boil, drain the water, and pound in the mortar until soft. Add hot spices, pour in tail fat, and cook in a brass pan until it contracts and browns. Put in a frying pan—putting in a layer of noodles, a layer of pounded meat, a layer of boiled lentils and so on—until the pan is full. Pour on a good quantity of melted fat and a little of the meat broth. Put the fat on it while it is on a low fire—pouring along the edges, using a thin ladle, so that the fat reaches underneath. Keep boiling till the noodles are done, and it is ready to eat. 6.126

THIRD RECIPE[34]

FOURTH RECIPE, CALLED *MUJADDARAH* Boil meat and large meatballs made with rice and chickpeas. Fry the meat, return the 6.127

broth to it, and add lentils which have been boiled separately until done, along with whole chickpeas. Add noodles and cook until done, and ladle out. It is eaten with a soup spoon.

◆

6.128 **SECTION ON NOODLES** Cut noodles from a sheet of *sanbūsak* dough, which is better for this purpose than unleavened bread dough. After boiling meat and meatballs made with rice and chick-peas, fry them in fat, adding a bit of the broth and a lot of tail fat. Add the noodles and cook on a low fire until they are done and have cooked up separately in the fat, with none of the broth remaining. Ladle out in mounds. If you want to put eggs in the meatballs, boil the eggs, cloak them with the meat, and make large meatballs; put them in with the noodles. The pounded meat will not stick when you stuff it with the eggs unless you put a little chickpea flour in it, otherwise it will detach.

6.129 **SECTION ON *TABBĀLAH*** Fry meat in its own fat after boiling it, and make meatballs, both with eggs and without, with rice and chickpeas in them. Add to the pot as described in making noodles, except that you put in rice before the noodles. Bring to the boil several times until done. Add ribs of chard and coriander leaves. If you wish, top the *tabbālah* with kebabs, *sanbūsak*, fried hard-boiled eggs, fried chicken, an egg cake, a sweetmeat, or the like, except that if it has a slack consistency, you consume it with a soup spoon instead of garnishing it.

Section on couscous, of which there are two types

6.130 **THE FIRST IS "BARLEYCORN" PASTA** Knead dough with yeast and twist it like barley grains. Put meat broth on them and boil until done. Strain off the water, pour plenty of tail fat on the pasta, leave on a quiet fire, and ladle out. Arrange meat and meatballs and so forth on top. Cook so that the grains separate, as with noodles. Add chickpeas.

THE SECOND TYPE IS NORTH AFRICAN COUSCOUS Spray water on flour and rub with your hand like for *mufattalah*. Sieve to take out the granules that form and set the small ones aside, repeating until you have as much as you want. Boil meat, meatballs, and chicken in a pot. Put what you have sieved out into a strainer or couscous steamer and cover it with a lid sealed with dough so that absolutely none of the steam escapes; the couscous cooks in the steam. When it is done, pour fat and clarified butter on it, rub with the hand, then moisten with broth, and ladle out. Arrange the meat, meatballs, and chicken on top, garnish with various kinds of garnishes, and serve the diners. 6.131

◆

MAʿSHŪQAH Cut 2 kg of boneless meat into small pieces and boil until half done. Strain the water. Fry with 1⅓ kg of tail fat cut in small pieces, the same size as the meat, and fry everything half done so that the pieces of fat are browned. Take 4 kg of good dates, their pits removed and replaced with pistachios, and sugar, musk, rose water, and honey. Arrange the dates on the fat and the meat, and leave on a low fire until the dates are done. Sprinkle with whole peeled pistachios, musk, and rose water, and remove and serve. If you wish, add hardboiled egg yolks. 6.132

***BADĪʿIYYAH*, A NORTH AFRICAN DISH** Fry meat brown and make small spiced meatballs. Take *khaysī* cheese (that is, the kind that can be fried). Bring water to a strong boil for it, cut the cheese up, throw in, and leave a while. Dry in a sieve and fry in sesame oil. Arrange the meat and cheese in a pan. Beat eggs with hot spices, minced parsley, and a little saffron. Use both the yolks and whites, but set some yolks aside. Pour the eggs with the hot spices and flavorings on the meat and the cheese, so that they cloak it all. Add a little 6.133

broth and a lot of tail fat, and leave on the fire until done. Put the reserved yolks on top, arrange the meatballs, the fried cheese, and the rest on it, then remove and serve.

Section on Apricots, Two Recipes

6.134 **The First Recipe** Boil fresh apricots until they fall apart and thicken while boiling with a piece of bread or a handful of pounded rice. Strain and put into a pot. Add pieces of fat meat and leave on the fire until half done. Add ribs of chard, mint, whole onions, and whole unpeeled heads of garlic. Make large meatballs with rice, crushed chickpeas, and pepper. Leave in the pan until the meat is fully cooked and falling apart, then ladle out. If it isn't sour enough, add lemon juice.

6.135 **Second Recipe, Dried Apricots** Cut meat in small pieces, boil, and set the broth aside. Fry the meat with onions, coriander leaves, and spices until done and the meat is reddish brown. Make sure to use plenty of onion. Take dried sweet-kerneled apricots, wash them in hot water a while, and remove their pits, taking care that none of the flesh comes away with a pit. Put them on the fried meat, add a little broth to cover, and cook uncovered for a little while such that the apricots do not disintegrate. When done, add honey and lemon juice; if you have sour grape juice, better yet as the flavor will be sweet-tart. Cook until the broth dries up. Add mint, coriander leaves, and onions. If you do not put lemon juice, add a little sour grape juice to strengthen it instead. Put in small meatballs with spices, mint, coriander leaves, and onions. Cook on a low fire, and ladle out. Sprinkle with coriander seeds and minced coriander leaves. If you have apricot leather from Byzantium or from Medina, that is better than dried apricots.

Section on bananas, for which there are three recipes

THE FIRST RECIPE Peel plantains,[35] cut lengthwise like taros, and fry in plenty of sesame oil so that the plantains brown and come out like taro. Cut up meat, boil, and fry as in the taro dish with coriander leaves, pounded garlic, and onions. When the meat is browned and done, add the fried plantains, some broth, and peeled hazelnuts, toasted and pounded smooth (I have described how to do this elsewhere in the book). Shake the pan until the broth dries up, ladle out, and serve. It resembles *sitt al-shunaʿ* in color and taste. 6.136

SECOND RECIPE Fry bananas and put them in thick syrup. Add pistachios. 6.137

***THIRD RECIPE** Use the lean meat of a small lamb, the same quantity of tail fat, a little Chinese cinnamon and mastic, and a little water, enough to cover everything. Cook and remove the scum. When nearly done, strain off the water, and fry in the fat. Meanwhile, prepare toasted pistachios and hazelnuts, one part each, two parts sugar, and a little saffron. Pound everything and mix with rose water. Take half and sprinkle on the meat in the pot. Then remove from the fire and arrange ripe yellow bananas on top, sprinkle with the rest of the sugar and nuts, and spray with a little rose water. Cover and allow to settle on the fire. Remove and serve. Do not let the fire get too hot. 6.138

Chapter 7

The Many Kinds of Sweets, Baked Goods, and the Like

7.1 **THE FIRST KIND IS *SANBŪSAK*** Take a sheet of *sanbūsak* dough, trim the edges,[36] spray with rose water, and sprinkle with finely pounded sugar. Fold the corners to the center and sprinkle with sugar, and crimp together in that way to make it the size of a large flat cake. Then take sesame oil, heat in the pan, and lay the cake in it, corners and upper surface protruding, until it firms up in frying. Then turn over and repeat until it has browned like a *sanbūsak*. Put in a dish, pour on thick syrup, and sprinkle with crushed toasted pistachios. The key is careful folding.

7.2 **THE SECOND KIND, WHICH IS EVEN BETTER THAN THE PERSIAN SWEET** Take 1 kg of finest white flour. Add ⅔ kg of clarified butter and toast on a charcoal fire until browned and fragrant. At this stage, have 1 kg of very finely ground sugar at hand. Take the pan from the fire, sprinkle with the sugar, and stir vigorously on the ground. When thoroughly mixed, set down a large iron pan, wiped clean, and pour in the toasted flour. Flatten with a smaller pan to smooth out and leave to cool a little. Cut with a broad-bladed knife into pieces of any size; peel off with the knife, lift pieces with the knife, arrange in rows on another pan or a dish, and leave to get cold. Sprinkle with sugar ground very finely with 1/20 g or more of musk, which gives a pleasant effect. Loose flour that cools in the pan will not cohere and combine like the rest, so return it to the first pan, at the lowest possible temperature that will make it unite and cohere. Flatten in the pan and repeat the process until the flour is used up. The proportion is 2 kg of sugar and 1⅓ kg of clarified butter for every 2 kg of flour. This is a dish that is delicious in wintertime.

THE THIRD KIND, *ṬARĀṬĪR AL-TURKUMĀN Take finest white flour. Knead with water, without salt, and roll out with a rolling pin. Cut into circles with a glass cup, bring two edges of each circle to the center and pinch together.[37] Boil sesame oil and stick the edges into it until they stiffen, then fry until brown. Stuff with pistachios, sugar, musk, and rose water, and sprinkle with sugar. 7.3

THE FOURTH KIND, *AL-MAKSHŪFAH* Pound 2 kg of peeled blanched almonds until they swim in their oil. Take 2 kg of white honey, 2 kg of sesame oil, and 2 kg of sieved, finely pounded sugar. Color the almonds with saffron and rose water, put in the sesame oil on a low fire, and toast well. When toasted, pour the sugar and honey on them, and cook until thick. Remove and serve, either in a dish or flattened out in a pan. The proportion is equal quantities. 7.4

THE FIFTH KIND, *MAʾMŪNIYYAH*, FOR WHICH THERE ARE THREE RECIPES

THE FIRST RECIPE Take a piece of tail fat and boil it in water until fully cooked and falling apart. Strain the water from it, macerate, and force through a sieve into a bowl. Wash rice, pound, and put through a fine sieve. Grind Egyptian sugar and put it with the rice and fat in a pan.[38] Cook on low fire until done and thickened. Spread out in a dish and top with whole blanched peeled pistachios. 7.5

THE SECOND RECIPE, BETTER THAN THE FIRST Wash and dry rice, pound fine, and sieve. Take boiled, clot-free fresh milk, put 7.6

on the fire, and add sugar so that it dissolves. Sprinkle with the rice and cook as a thin pudding. Add a good bit of melted tail fat; the pudding will absorb the fat. Keep cooking on a low fire until the fat is released, which indicates that it is done. Cook the rice until golden brown and add peeled pistachios. When thick enough, spread out in plates and garnish with fresh pistachios, pomegranate seeds, and colored hard candies.

7.7 **THE THIRD RECIPE, WHICH IS BETTER THAN THE SECOND** Boil fattened chickens and fry in sesame oil. Take the breasts and separate into threads. Wash rice, pound fine, and sieve. On every 2 kg of rice put the shredded breasts of two chickens and enough sugar to sweeten to taste. Then take milk, boil, and dissolve the sugar to make it extremely sweet. Add the chicken breasts and bring to the boil two or three times, then sprinkle with the rice and stir so that it doesn't set. When the mixture is like porridge, or a little more liquid than that, add tail fat. Keep cooking on a low fire until it exudes fat and turns brown. And keep stirring till it can be spread out in a dish. Ladle out and put whole peeled pistachios in the middle. By incorporating chicken breasts, it turns out very nicely. This is how it is done in the house of my uncle, al-Malik al-Ashraf.

THE SIXTH KIND, PISTACHIO PORRIDGE, FOR WHICH THERE ARE THREE RECIPES

7.8 **THE FIRST RECIPE** Blanch pistachios, peel off the outer skin, dry off, roast on a low fire, and pound smooth until they swim in their oil. For every 2 kg of pistachios, use two breasts of chicken. Boil the chickens without salt and fry in good olive oil. Cool, remove the bones, and tease the meat into threads as delicately as possible. If you can use a needle, even better. When you have shredded some meat, wrap in chard leaves so that it stays moist. Then dissolve sugar to make a thin, half-thickened syrup. Add the chicken breast and stir with a dowel so that it does not clump. When the chicken breast has browned to the right degree but has not dried out, add the pistachios described earlier and beat the mixture with a ladle, the way you beat meat porridge, until thick. Add starch dissolved with rose water. For every 2 kg of pistachios, add ¼ kg of good honey and also the fat that came out of the chickens in cooking. While adding these, put in enough chard puree to color the dish as green as you want. Scent with musk and rose water, spread out in dishes, and garnish with hard candies and sugar.

THE SECOND RECIPE, ḤIMMAṢIYYAH This is made the same way as the first, but with peeled green chickpeas (*ḥimmaṣ*) instead of pistachios. 7.9

THE THIRD RECIPE, FISTIQIYYAH WITHOUT CHICKEN Take pistachios, blanch, roast, and pound until they swim in their oil, as you do in making pistachio porridge. Thicken syrup, add the pistachios and starch, cook until done and thickened, and it is ready to use. To color it green, use chard puree. 7.10

THE SEVENTH KIND, MADE WITH DATES Pit dates. Take blanched, peeled, and ground pistachios, and make into a paste with sugar, rose water, and musk. Use to stuff the dates. Take crepe batter and add starch dissolved in rose water—add it in thoroughly dissolved form, as you do when making *zulabiyyah* fritter batter. Dip the dates into the batter, fry in sesame oil, and put into thick syrup. Then dip back into the batter, fry again, and put in syrup. Arrange on a plate, sprinkle with sugar and pistachios, and spray with rose water and musk. 7.11

THE EIGHTH KIND, *AL-MARĪS* Remove pits from the dates. Take sieved *kumāj* bread crumbs and as much sesame oil, fresh butter, clarified butter, or tail fat as you want. Put the fat in a pan, add the dates and cook until they disintegrate, then add the bread crumbs and stir well. Sprinkle with enough sugar to make it distinctly sweet, add crushed roasted pistachios, and ladle into serving plates. 7.12

7.13 **THE NINTH KIND, *AL-MAKHNŪQAH*** Rub fine white flour with clarified butter or tail fat and knead firmly with sourdough. Use a rolling pin to roll out like pasta squares, leave to rise, and fry in sesame oil until light brown. Cook the sweetmeat *ṣābūniyyah* with whole pistachios, and when nearly done add the fried pastry sheets and stir with an iron paddle. Spread out on serving dishes. This is very tasty.

7.14 **THE TENTH KIND, *NĀṢIRIYYAH*, WHICH USED TO BE MADE IN THE HOUSE OF AL-MALIK AL-NĀṢIR, THE GOVERNOR OF ALEPPO, MAY GOD SHOWER MERCY UPON HIM** Take fine white flour and knead it as described earlier. Roll out thin with a rolling pin, cut into round shapes with a ravioli mold, and fry in sesame oil until browned. Make *ṣābūniyyah* sweetmeat and stick a piece of it between every two fried pastries. Sprinkle with sugar and pistachios.

7.15 **A SIMILAR VARIATION** For every 2 kg of flour, take ⅚ kg of clarified butter or tail fat. Knead with a good deal of yeast and leave to rise. Make into thin cakes, as thin as possible, and stamp out with a cookie mold. Bake in the oven and put as much *ṣābūniyyah* between the cakes as you like.

7.16 **THE ELEVENTH KIND** Toast flour with clarified butter until done. Take from the fire, work in sugar, and knead into shapes like breasts. Put in a tray and put in the oven until baked and done. If you do not bake them, they will run. Use equal parts flour and butter.

7.17 **THE TWELFTH KIND, *AL-KĀHĪN*** For every egg white, take 6⅓ g of starch. Grind starch fine, put in a cup with the egg white, add a little rose water, not too much, and let dissolve. Take a new whisk made of matting straw and beat the egg white and starch until thoroughly mixed and foamy. Set a frying pan on a low fire. When the sesame oil is hot, spoon some egg white and starch into it by droplets and fry till brown. Do not let any stick together. Do not put in big droplets; small ones will grow larger in the pan. Remove from the pan and put into syrup thickened to the thread stage. Eat them hot, because they are no longer good when they get cold. They taste better fried in clarified butter instead of sesame oil.

A VARIATION[39] Blanch pistachios, pound smooth with sugar, and knead into rings with rose water. Pick them up on a dowel, immerse in the egg white and starch mixture made for *kahin*, and stir until the pistachio rings are coated. Panfry and put into syrup. This is a nice dish. 7.18

THE THIRTEENTH KIND, HORSEHIDE, ALSO KNOWN AS "STARCH SLURRY" Fry starch slurry in sesame oil, put into syrup, and sprinkle with sugar. It is a nice dish. 7.19

THE FOURTEENTH KIND, *KUNĀFAH MAMLŪḤAH* Take *kunāfah* flatbread, rub with sesame oil, fold into layers, and grease with sesame oil between every two layers. Cut it into thin noodles. Put in a dish and moisten with sesame oil, pounded sugar, and toasted pistachios. 7.20

ANOTHER VERSION Once you have cut the flatbread into noodles with sesame oil, moisten in the dish with butter and sprinkle with sugar, pistachios, and syrup. Butter gives a more delicious result than sesame oil, but when cutting you must use sesame oil. 7.21

ANOTHER VERSION Blanch pistachios, pound with sugar, and knead with rose water. Take flatbreads greased with sesame oil, put the pistachios on them, roll them up, and cut the rolls into pieces. Moisten with fresh sesame oil and syrup thickened to the thread stage. 7.22

ANOTHER VARIETY Take flatbread, fry in sesame oil, put in syrup, and sprinkle with sugar and pistachios. 7.23

7.24 ***ANOTHER VARIETY, KNOWN AS *AKHMĪMIYYAH*** Cut up 2 kg of flatbread, put in the pan with 500 g of sesame oil, and fry a little. Then add 2 kg of crushed sugar and continue to fry until the bread releases the sesame oil it absorbed. This is the sign that it is fried enough. Add ⅔ kg of honey, stir, then add ⅔ kg of pounded toasted hazelnuts. Take from the fire, perfume with musk and rose water, and set aside. This variety will last a year without deteriorating. The longer it sits, the better it tastes.

THE FIFTEENTH KIND, CREPES, OF WHICH THERE ARE SEVERAL TYPES

7.25 **THE FIRST TYPE** Blanch pistachios, dry them out, toast on a low fire, pound, and knead with finely ground sugar and rose water. After stuffing the crepes with this mixture, extract a little pistachio oil (better than sesame oil) and moisten the crepes with it. Serve in syrup.

7.26 **THE SECOND TYPE** Use oil extracted from toasted walnuts instead of sesame oil.

7.27 ***THE THIRD TYPE, FRIED CREPES** Knead together musk, rose water, 2 kg of sugar, ⅙ kg of flour, and ½ kg of peeled almonds or pistachios. Use this mixture to stuff the crepes. Seal them with batter, fry, and serve in syrup cooked with honey to the thread stage.[40]

7.28 ***THE FOURTH TYPE, JAMĀLIYYAH CREPES** Put sugar, pistachios, rose water, and musk on a large round crepe and cover it with another. Seal the edges with dough, fry in sesame oil, and remove from the pan when still somewhat moist. Serve in syrup, honey, and rose water.

7.29 **A TYPE CALLED ABŪ LĀSH** One variety of *abū lāsh* crepes is made with milk and sugar, and another is small round crepes sprinkled with crushed toasted pistachios. Pour syrup on top.

A TYPE CALLED EAT AND GIVE THANKS, ALSO CALLED QARNI YĀRŪQ[41] Knead flour with clarified butter, then knead with water and roll out with a dowel as you do pasta. Melt clarified butter, grease the pasta sheets with it, and fold them over to make (double) layers four fingers wide. Cut into rectangles and fry in sesame oil until light brown. Put in a dish and sprinkle with sugar, pistachios, and syrup thickened to the thread stage. 7.30

ANOTHER TYPE Knead as described and roll out as described with clarified butter. Wrap around a dowel, stand it upright, and slide the pastry off it. Form into a cake and fry in sesame oil. Dress with sugar and syrup. 7.31

THE SIXTEENTH KIND, MADE TO LOOK LIKE MULBERRIES Rub flour with clarified butter and knead hard. Make the dough into a lump the size of a mulberry and put in a sieve. Put your finger in the middle of the lump and rub it around so that it hollows out and takes on the pattern of the sieve. Fry in sesame oil and put in syrup. It is quite tasty. The key to making it is using a sieve and putting plenty of butter in the dough. 7.32

THE SEVENTEENTH KIND, *FAṬĀʾIR* Rub dough with clarified butter, rubbing it hard and kneading stiff. Roll out with a dowel like pasta. Grease with butter inside and out and wrap around the dowel. Stand the dowel upright and twist the dough outward with the right hand and inward with the left. Carefully slip it off the dowel, flatten into a cake, and bake in the oven until toasted. When hot, drench with fresh butter and syrup. 7.33

THE EIGHTEENTH KIND, BASRA-STYLE *BASĪSAH* Make unleavened dough as above and bake in the oven. When cold, break up, crush, and put through a sieve. Moisten with rose water, sugar, pistachios, and clarified or fresh butter. 7.34

7.35 **THE NINETEENTH KIND, *KASHK* SWEETMEAT** Take freshly made *kashk*.[42] Make syrup, add the *kashk*, and thicken on a low fire. It comes out as a digestible dish for invalids. To make it more tart, add lemon juice.

7.36 **THE TWENTIETH KIND, A GOOD SWEETMEAT KNOWN AS *MAKKIYYAH*** Take 120 g of starch and 120 g of semolina. Mix and sieve. Put 360 g of tail fat or sesame oil on the fire. When boiling hot, sprinkle with the flour and starch, then bring to the boil two or three times more. Pour in skimmed honey or strong syrup and cook until thick. Spread out on a plate, top with pistachios, and sprinkle with sugar.

7.37 **ANOTHER VARIETY** Take 360 g of starch, 240 g of milk, and 6 g of saffron. Dissolve and knead with 60 g of the milk. Add the whites of seven eggs and put through a sieve after mixing. Add the remaining 180 g of milk. Thicken syrup to the thread stage. Heat sesame oil in frying pan. Dip your hand in the batter and shake your fingers into the pan, scattering drops. As they brown, remove and put in syrup, until the batter is used up.

Supplement on sweets—
not part of the original book

7.38 **BREAD *JŪDHĀB*** Soak crumbs of leavened bread in milk until it sours. Put sugar and pounded almonds colored with saffron over and under. Leave on the fire until fragrant, then remove and serve.

7.39 **CREPE *JŪDHĀB*** Arrange crepes stuffed with almonds and sugar syrup between two thin flatbreads in a pan. Set beneath a chicken in the clay oven, putting almonds and sugar, finely pounded and spiced as for crepe stuffing, between the layers. Pour on sesame oil and milk, and more sugar if you wish. When done and fragrant, remove and serve.

BANANA *JŪDHĀB* Take firm yellow bananas. Peel and immerse them in thin semolina dough which has been kneaded like crepe batter. Then remove and fry in sesame oil on a low fire. Remove, dip in syrup, and lay in pounded sugar. Arrange in a pan with thin flatbreads over and under, and set in a clay oven beneath a fat hen. 7.40

MELON *JŪDHĀB* Made the same way as banana *jūdhāb*. 7.41

CREPE BREAD Take as many crepes as you need. Sprinkle a little rose water in the pan and arrange the crepes in layers, with almonds and sugar or finely pounded pistachios between every two layers, and sprinkle rose water on top. When the pan is full, pour on a little fresh sesame oil and cover with syrup. Set in a clay oven, hang a fat chicken colored with saffron above it, and remove when done. You can make small stuffed crepes according to this recipe, except that you hang the chicken over a pan of water, and when the chicken is nearly done and its fat about to drip, remove the pan of water and put the pan containing the *jūdhāb* under it. 7.42

POPPY-SEED *JŪDHĀB* Make 4 kg of sugar into thin syrup. Add 1 kg of semolina, ½ kg of pistachios, and 1 kg of poppy seeds. Color with saffron and thicken on the fire, adding honey if you want. When thickened, put between two thin flatbreads and hang a fat hen colored with saffron over it in the clay oven. 7.43

ALMOND PUDDING Made the same way, except that the poppy seeds are replaced with blanched almonds, minced and pounded smooth.[43] 7.44

DATE *JŪDHĀB* Put 8 kg of dates in a pan of water and kindle a fire under it until done. Macerate well with the hand and filter through a strainer. Then return the date paste to the pan and add 1 kg of sugar, 2 kg of honey, 1½ g of saffron, 2 kg of crumbled bread, and 2 kg of sesame oil, all at once. Stir with an iron paddle until it casts off fat. 7.45

Add a handful of poppy seeds and 1 kg of pistachios if you like. Then ladle it out, put pounded sugar over and under, and dispatch.[44]

7.46 ***SAMĪDHIYYAH*** Toast 2 kg of semolina with 2 kg of sesame oil and stir until fragrant. Add 8 kg of syrup or honey and cook on a low fire. Stir with an iron paddle until it gives off oil, then set aside. Roll in sugar and spice with camphor.

7.47 **MARZIPAN** Take 2 kg of pounded peeled sweet almonds and 6 kg of sugar. Pound the sugar and put in a pan without water. When it melts, add the almonds and thicken. Roll out and cut into pieces. If you wish, add two *ūqiyah*s of starch to make it pleasantly crisp. Flavor with a little rose water and a lot of musk before adding the starch.

7.48 **GOURD PUDDING** Peel gourds, clean them out, boil in syrup, and set to drain on a woven tray. Grind in a stone mortar and squeeze out in the hand. Then put sesame oil in a pan; after it boils, add starch and then the gourds, and moisten with syrup. Cook until it thickens and set aside. Add pounded peeled pistachios and color with chard puree. You make a carrot version the same way, except that it is not colored with the chard puree.

7.49 ***AL-MUKHANNAQAH*** Take 4 kg of thin flatbread, 2 kg of sugar, 3 kg of honey, ⅔ kg of sesame oil and ⅔ kg of pistachios. Dissolve half the sugar in water and pound the other half. Boil the honey with the sugar syrup and add the flatbread. Moisten the ingredients with sesame oil, stir around so that they mix, and take down from the fire. Pound the pistachios and add to the pounded half of the sugar. Sprinkle them on the syrup-bread mixture, bring to the boil, and scent with musk and rose water.

7.50 ***AL-RĀWANDĪ*** Grind starch and sieve it. Boil honey until it is thickened to the thread stage. Work in the starch, then form it into rings and put one into boiling sesame oil. If it rises, good; if not, increase the starch. When fried, put in lukewarm honey.

LETTUCE PUDDING Take lettuce leaves trimmed of their bases and tips, peel, cut up, and boil in syrup (sc. and remove). Take starch and dissolve with a little of the syrup which the lettuce has been boiled in. Pound poppy seeds, put everything in the syrup, and stir around with some sesame oil. When done, add the boiled lettuce, stir, and add spices, then remove and serve. 7.51

MAIDENS' CHEEKS Knead 4 kg of flour and 4½ g of starch with 12 g of sesame oil; add a little syrup while kneading. Roll out, cut into circles with a cup, and prick them in the middle so that they won't puff up. Put in a frying pan on a low fire, then turn over. Put in syrup and honey, take out, cover with the sweetmeat called *ṣābūniyyah*, and sprinkle with sugar. 7.52

ASYŪṬIYYAH Sieve 1 kg of day-old bread crumbs. Take musk, rose water, ⅔ kg of honey, 1 kg of syrup, ⅙ kg of poppy seeds, ⅙ kg of pistachios, 1 kg of dates, and ⅓ kg of almonds colored with 3 g of saffron. Combine everything with the bread crumbs and put the mixture between two thin flatbreads. Melt ⅔ kg of tail fat without salt in ⅔ kg of sesame oil, ⅓ kg of it in its filling and ⅓ kg with the tail fat.[45] Then pour the tail fat and sesame oil on the *asyūṭiyyah*. Put in a pot and set in the clay oven until well done, then remove and serve. 7.53

NĀṬIF Thicken dissolved sugar or honey on a low fire until a sample taken out will crack and shatter. Knead with it whatever flavoring you wish, such as sesame seeds, pistachios, almonds, hazelnuts, or chickpeas.[46] Then remove and serve. 7.54

PURSLANE-SEED SWEETMEAT This is made just like poppy-seed sweetmeat.[47] 7.55

7.56 ***SHAYZARIYYAH*** Fry ⅔ kg of bread crumbs in ⅓ kg of sesame oil. Add ⅓ kg of nuts and 1/12 kg of poppy seeds, fry together, and set aside. Make a syrup; let it thicken and put in one-sixth as much of honey. Add the bread crumbs, nuts, and poppy seeds you have set aside, stir, and flavor with musk and rose water.

7.57 **TAFFY** Dissolve sugar in a pan. To every 4 kg add ½ kg of rose water. Cook on a low fire until it is chewy if you take some and put in your mouth. Leave a little, put on a smooth stone tile, and knead with about ⅙ kg of crushed peeled almonds or pistachios. Allow to cool and set aside. If you wish, work in both kinds of nut, or add hazelnuts and bejeweled chickpeas;[48] it comes out nicely. If you wish, color the taffy with a little saffron before removing from the fire. You can also pound almonds fine and mix in. If you wish, take the taffy from the tile and stretch it on an iron peg driven into the wall until it turns white, then knead with peeled pistachios and make into cakes and figures and so on. If you want, color with saffron or cinnamon bark or anything else you want when it is on the fire. One variety is kneaded with toasted sesame seeds or poppy seeds, and made into figures in the same way.

7.58 ***ḤALWĀʾ TAMRIYYAH*** Thicken *ṣābūniyyah* as usual, add date paste, and stir. Add pistachios, hazelnuts, or poppy seeds. Use plenty of honey, and color with saffron. It is delicious.

7.59 **A DELICIOUS ROSE *ḤALWĀʾ*** Boil roses in water until it takes their color, then add syrup. Cook until properly thick and moisten slowly with rose water. When nearly set, dissolve starch as usual with rose water and add to syrup/rose syrup, then add some fresh rose petals. Take some sesame oil and stir it in. Add pistachios, and scent with musk and rose water.

7.60 ***ṢĀBŪNIYYAH*** Dissolve sugar and set aside. Put half the syrup in the pan, dissolve starch, add to the syrup, and stir continuously on the fire; for 2 kg of sugar, use ⅙ kg of starch. Stir with sesame oil, slowly moisten with the rest of the syrup, and stir. When it comes off the fire, add honey, the same amount by weight as the starch. When done, set aside and work in, for every 2 kg, ⅓ kg of blanched almonds or pistachios and ⅙ kg of rose water. Then spread it out and sprinkle with sugar.

A FINE SWEETMEAT Stir 4 kg of sugar, 1 kg of honey, 1 kg of 7.61
sesame oil, and ⅔ kg of starch on the fire until medium thick. Spread out[49] in a thin sheet and top with a filling of ⅔ kg of sugar, ½ kg of finely pounded pistachios, musk, and rose water, then cover with another coat of the sweetmeat and cut into pieces. It is extremely delicious. If you wish, form the filling into mouthful-sized balls and wrap them in the sweetmeat; this is called *sabʿīniyyah.*

MARZIPAN Pound one part almonds coarsely and add an equal 7.62
amount of finely pounded sugar along with a third as much of rose water, and dissolve on the fire. When thickened, add more sugar and take it from the fire. This is dry marzipan.

FOR THE MOIST VERSION take 2 kg of sugar and ⅔ kg of peeled 7.63
blanched almonds and grind both fine. Mix the almonds with the sugar and knead with rose water. Take bread dough rolled thin as for *sanbūsak*, the thinner the better; the most suitable sort is *kunāfah* flatbread.[50] Spread out a sheet of that dough and put the kneaded almond and sugar filling on it, then roll up, cut in small pieces, and arrange in rows in a vessel. Take as much fresh sesame oil as necessary and add, then cover with syrup dissolved with rose water. Scatter sugar and finely pounded pistachios on top and use.

You can make another variety, as follows. Take starch, knead 7.64
firmly with water, and when stiff, carefully thin it out to the consistency of milk.[51] Take a pastry tray.[52] Heat it, pour batter on it using a dribbler, and remove when cooked. Roll up pistachios, sugar, musk,

and rose water in the pastry, arrange the rolls side by side, and cut into pieces. Add hot sesame oil and syrup and sprinkle with sugar. This is to be eaten right away. If kept overnight, it goes bad.

7.65 **ZAYNAB'S FINGERS** Rub 4 kg of flour with ½ kg of sesame oil. Then knead with hot water and put on a length of Persian cane, daubing it on, and fry with the cane. Remove from the oil and extract the cane. Stuff the fried pastry tube with sugar, pistachios, musk, and rose water; put in honey; and sprinkle with sugar.

7.66 ***FĀLŪDHAJ*** Toast bread crumbs in sesame oil and add a little milk. When the milk has nearly dried up, thicken with syrup and honey. When taking it down from the fire, add pounded sugar and pistachios and put musk and rose water on it.

7.67 **DRY *FĀLŪDHAJ*** Take 2 kg of sugar and ⅔ kg of almonds or pistachios; pound smooth and flavor with musk, camphor, and rose water. Take ⅔ kg of sugar and melt on a low fire with 1⁄12 kg of rose water. Set aside, and when it cools, add the sugar and pounded almonds and knead together. If it needs to be firmer, add more sugar and almonds and knead hard. Make into roll-ups, figures, and other shapes. Then remove and serve.

7.68 ***MUKAFFAN*** Grind 2 kg of sugar and 1 kg of almonds and fortify with a little flour. Knead some more flour with ½ kg of sesame oil to every 2 kg of the flour along with as much water as needed. Roll out, cut into pieces, stuff, and fry on a low fire. Dip in syrup and sprinkle with sugar.

7.69 **A BETTER VERSION OF *MUKAFFAN*** Pound together one part sugar and one-third part pistachios or almonds and knead stiffly with musk and rose water. Put ⅙ kg of sesame oil in the pan and dissolve 2 kg of sugar to make syrup. When the sesame oil boils, put a third of the syrup on it and stir continuously. Add starch dissolved in water and stir continuously[53] until nearly set. Moisten with the rest of the syrup, stir, and pour onto a smooth tile to cool. Roll out, cut into smooth little mouthful-sized pieces, put some of that kneaded sugar-and-almond (or -pistachio) paste on them, and make into roll-ups. Sprinkle with sugar, and remove and serve.

MUSHABBAK Mix one part starch with two parts sourdough, and thin with hot water to the thickness of yogurt. Test by putting some in boiling sesame oil; if it rises and floats on top, good. If it doesn't, increase the quantity of sourdough. Once you have tested it, take a coconut shell pierced at the bottom, put your finger over the hole, and fill with batter. Put sesame oil in the pan, and when it boils, remove your finger and move your hand around to form round lattices. Take out and put in syrup. 7.70

QĀHIRIYYAH Finely grind two parts sugar and one part pistachios. Knead with rose water and musk, add an eighth as much flour as their total weight, make into rings and cakes, and leave them on a pan overnight to dry. Take two parts flour and one part starch and knead a little firmer than *mushabbak* batter. Dip the rings and cakes in the batter, fry, and put into hot syrup mixed with honey. Then remove and serve. 7.71

THE PERSIAN SWEET Take very finely ground flour, and equal amounts of sesame oil and honey. The best way to make it is to put sesame oil on a charcoal fire until it boils strongly, then sprinkle with the flour, and stir. The sign that it is well toasted is if a drop of honey is dripped in it, it will float on top. When done and fragrant, clarify honey on another fire and add saffron. When it boils, pour on the flour and stir. Add pistachios or almonds colored with saffron and cover for a good while so that the vapors don't escape. Remove the cover, flavor with rose water and musk, and sprinkle with sugar. Add cleaned poppy seeds, then remove and serve. 7.72

7.73 **FISH AND CAKES** Take 3 kg of sugar and 1 kg of almonds. Peel the almonds, pound smooth, and flavor with a little musk. Take 1 kg of honey and put in the pan with ⅙ kg of rose water until it boils. Remove the scum. Then take ⅙ kg of starch dissolved with rose water, add to the honey, and stir awhile until it has the proper consistency. Add the pounded sugar and almonds, and beat vigorously with an iron paddle until it sets. Then take from the fire and leave on a smooth tile to cool off. Use carved molds to make it into fish, cakes, and other shapes, and sprinkle with finely ground sugar and pistachios. Color the fish with a little saffron moistened with rose water, then remove and serve.

7.74 **STUFFED FRITTERS** Knead a stiff dough of flour with leaven. Roll out and stuff with sugar and almonds scented with rose water, musk, and camphor. Form in a mold of any shape desired, then leave awhile to dry. Dip in fritter batter, then put in fresh sesame oil and fry. Dip in syrup, remove, and dust with sugar.

7.75 **PISTACHIO PORRIDGE** Put sieved crumbs of day-old bread in a pan. Add sesame oil and moisten crumbs until they ooze. Then add 2 kg of syrup and 2 kg of honey separately, moistening first with the syrup then with the honey. Stir and add 1 kg of pistachios. Take chicken breasts washed in rose water, five chicken breasts for every 2 kg of syrup. Add the breasts, then the honey (sc. and syrup and crumbs), and cook until the syrup thickens and will pour from the ladle in a long thread. Add pistachios and stir as for *ṣābūniyyah*. If it turns yellow, color it with chard puree or indigo in the sesame oil. Spice, remove, and sprinkle with spiced sugar. Make sure the chicken breasts used were boiled and separated into threads.

7.76 **FROSTED COOKIES** These are similar to *khushkanānaj* cookies and their stuffing. The difference here is that you take 1 kg of sugar, sprinkle it on the syrup, boil continuously until properly thickened, and empty it into a vessel. When the cookies come out of the oven hot, dip them in it so that it will congeal on them. Sprinkle with spiced sugar.

STUFFED CREPES Throw oblong crepes and stuff them with pistachios or almonds, and sugar, musk, and rose water, kneaded with a little syrup or honey, or both. When stuffed, roll up and arrange side by side in a dish. Add sesame oil, strong syrup, whole blanched pistachios, and toasted hazelnuts along with twice as much sugar. You can knead the sugar with honey if you wish, and you can also add untoasted flour to the stuffing, an eighth as much as the sugar, along with musk and rose water. This is also suitable as a filling for the fried version, which is as follows: Stuff crepes, seal with dough, fry, and put in syrup or honey. 7.77

The way to make crepe batter is to knead unleavened dough by itself, then dilute sourdough with hot water and a little baker's borax or roasted natron, which they call "spices." Put some sourdough on the unleavened dough and stir a while. If it rises well, good. If not, add more sourdough with the described "spices." *Kunāfah* flatbread is unleavened.

THE HONEYCOMB Put semolina flour through a fine sieve and rub well with sesame oil. Knead with water as needed and leave awhile. Then roll out a sheet of dough, a span by a span in size. Take the same filling of almonds and sugar as in the previous recipe, divide in equal proportions, and use to fill the dough. Cover with another sheet and pinch them together around the filling. Put in the clay oven until done on both sides. Put in a tray and pour thickened clarified honey on top. Sprinkle with sugar and pistachios spiced with musk and rose water. 7.78

***AQRĀṢ MUKARRARAH*, TRIPLE-DIPPED COOKIES** Knead semolina flour moderately thin and let it rise. Take 2 kg of sugar and ⅔ kg of pistachios or almonds, pound together, and knead hard with rose water and syrup. Make into cakes, coat with the batter, and 7.79

fry. Immerse in syrup, dust with sugar, then return to the batter; remove, fry, immerse in the syrup, and dust with sugar. Do this three times. Sprinkle with sugar, then remove and serve.

7.80 ***AQRĀṢ MUKALLALAH*, DEEP-FRIED SWEETMEAT** Cut strongly thickened sweetmeat in pieces as for *sanbūsak*, put in crepe batter, and fry in sesame oil. Put in syrup, musk, and rose water.

7.81 ***AQRĀṢ SĀDHIJAH*, PLAIN CAKES** Grind starch and knead with sourdough. When it rises, make into cakes. Fry, put in syrup, and sprinkle with sugar.

7.82 ***LUQAM AL-QĀḌĪ*, THE JUDGE'S MORSEL** Knead 2 kg of flour with ⅓ kg of sesame oil and ⅙ kg of water, or a little more as needed. When it rises, take sugar and finely pounded pistachios or almonds, two-thirds sugar and one-third pistachios. Knead with rose water and musk or musked syrup, and make into as many bite-sized morsels as you like. Coat lightly with the batter, put in sesame oil, and fry. Dip in syrup, allow to dry, and dust with spiced sugar, then remove and serve.

7.83 ***AL-DINNAF*** Take syrup, scald it, then remove from the fire. Add an egg white and beat until it turns white. For every 2 kg of syrup, take ⅙ kg of blanched pistachios or almonds and 42 g of finely ground starch, mix together, roll out with a rolling pin, and add sesame seeds.

7.84 **MOSUL *KATĀ*** Toast flour by itself and rub it with tail fat until it resembles peppercorns. Use it to stuff another batch of flour which has been kneaded without leaven into the shape of an eagle.[54] Leave uncovered and bake in a clay oven or small underground oven. Take out hot and add honey, then serve.

EXCELLENT *QĀHIRIYYAH* Take 2 kg of sugar, ½ kg of almonds or pistachios, and ½ kg of special high-grade flour. Pound the sugar fine and strain through a wheat-flour sieve. Do likewise with the nuts. Then mix the ingredients and knead with ⅔ kg of sesame oil and as much as you need of rose water flavored with musk and camphor. Form into rings of any size you want. Sprinkle flour on a wooden board, put the rings on it, and leave them uncovered for a day and a night. Then take a vessel, put 3 kg of good sourdough in it, and beat well by hand to the consistency of fritter batter. Add 6 g of natron and ⅙ kg of ground starch and beat everything well. Add two or three egg whites and beat until it becomes like fritter batter. Prepare the pan with sesame oil, dip the rings in that batter, then fry, and remove. Put in honey and sprinkle with spiced sugar and pounded pistachios. 7.85

URNĪN Take excellent flour. To every 2 kg add ⅔ kg of sesame oil, ⅙ kg of sesame seeds, and a handful of pistachios and almonds. Wait until the dough rises, then make into cakes and bake until browned. This is *khubz al-abāzīr*. If you want to make the dough into *urnīn*, when it rises, take a round mold, make thin cakes, and shape in the mold. Fill the cakes with pounded sugar, pistachios, and almonds, the sugar being two parts and the pistachios and almonds one part; scent the filling with rose water, musk, and camphor. Firmly close up the tops, put in the oven, and remove when lightly browned. Some people knead dates with sesame oil, remove the pits, and add some spices to make a filling for those cakes. 7.86

HONEYED DATES Take freshly picked fully ripe dates and spread them out, shaded, in the open air for two days. Then remove the pits from the bottom with a sharpened stick or a pack needle, and in place of every pit put a peeled sweet almond. For every 10 kg of dates, take 20 kg of honey thinned with ⅙ kg of rose water. Put honey on the fire, skim off the foam, then color with 1½ g of saffron. Add the dates, and when it comes to the boil, stir lightly so that they absorb 7.87

the honey. Then remove from the fire and spread them out on a nice pan. When cool, sprinkle with spiced, finely pounded sugar. If you want it to heat the bodily humors, make with musk, spikenard, and some spices; if you want it to cool them, make with camphor and a bit of poppy seed. Store in glass vessels. They are only used in the cold season and when soft-ripe dates are unavailable.

7.88 **HOW TO MAKE SOFT-RIPE DATES OUT OF SEASON** Wet a piece of lining cloth, wring it out, and roll up whole dried dates in it overnight. Take a new earthenware jug and fill with water for that night. In the morning, remove the water and put the dates in the jug for another night. They will be good the next morning.

7.89 **ANOTHER GOOD VARIATION** Take as many large *muthmir* dry dates as desired, complete with their calyxes. Macerate in hot water a while, then wash and spread out to dry. Take a green melon, scoop out the top to a hand's depth and take out the core. Put the dates inside, cover, and leave them there for a day. Check on them until they are ready. Take out, put on a woven tray, line up, and sprinkle with sugar, rose water, and fresh sesame oil.

7.90 **STUFFED DATES** Wash large Iraqi *muthmir* dry dates in hot water. Remove their pits and replace with almonds or pistachios. Boil syrup and honey and skim off the foam. Add the dates, and when it has come to the boil, leave to cool. Color with saffron and flavor with musk and rose water. For best results the syrup should be well thickened. This is very tasty.

7.91 **FRIED PASTRY SHEETS** Put ⅓ kg of sesame oil in a tinned copper frying pan with vertical sides. When it boils, add ½ kg of honey. Then take 1 kg of semolina flour and mix with ¼ kg of peeled and pounded medium-sized almonds, pistachios, and hazelnuts, and ⅓ kg of finely pounded sugar. Sprinkle on the honey and stir until thickened and fragrant. If it needs to be stronger, add more flour.

Color with a bit of saffron dissolved in rose water. Take from the fire, spread out on a smooth tile, and cut it into pieces. Dip them in syrup, dust with spiced sugar, and remove and serve.

BASĪSAH Take day-old bread crumbs, put through a sieve, and rub by hand until they become like poppy seeds. For every 2 kg, have ⅙ kg of sesame oil boiling on the fire. Rub the crumbs well with the oil and sprinkle with ⅙ kg of finely pounded sugar, 55 g of poppy seeds, and a bit of toasted sesame seeds, then mix in a dish or on a tray. If you need to, make it sweeter with a little honey. Then sprinkle with 83 g of sugar and pistachios and set aside. 7.92

A reliable authority has informed me that when you have fresh green wheat grains, you should put them in a pot, cover it, and seal with clay. Set on a fire of embers for a little while so that the grains sweat, then remove them and spread out to dry. Then toast them and make into unleavened bread, or into *basīsah*. It comes out as delicious as can be. In other words, you rub the wheat grains from the ears without scorching first in the usual way. 7.93

QĀWŪT Semolina, ground toasted wheat, and ground rice in equal proportion. Knead everything with tail fat, sesame oil, and clarified butter, and toast on the fire. Have some heated honey ready. Add the toasted flour and put in toasted hazelnuts, almonds dyed with saffron, and finger-sized pieces of Khuzistani sugar. Rice can be used by itself if it is washed, ground, fried in clarified butter, then dried and ground again. For a delicious result, add an equal weight of sugar to the toasted grain and rub with a little clarified butter. 7.94

It is also good if you take washed rice, grind and toast it with tail fat or clarified butter, then boil honey, skim the foam, add sugar, and put the rice in the honey to cook until done. Add pistachios, hazelnuts, almonds, apple dough, lemon dough, and hard candies. Set aside and spice.

7.95 ***KHUSHKANĀNAJ* AND *BASANDŪD*** Take excellent flour. Use ⅓ kg of sesame oil for every *raṭl* (2 kg) and knead hard with a little water; do not add any sourdough. Then immediately form it into elongated cakes and put finely pounded sugar and almonds on top. The cakes should have a noticeable taste of spice, as much as desired. Use four parts sugar, two parts almonds, one part fine flour, and as much spice as you wish. Join the ends over the filling and bake in the oven. If you want them to be sweet, stuff, fry, then dip them in syrup.

Basandūd is *khushkanānaj* dough made into flat cakes. Prick them so that they won't puff up and bake in the oven, then put some plain sweetmeat between every two cakes. There is no harm in putting almonds and pistachios in the sweetmeat.

[End of Supplement]

Baked goods

7.96 We begin with several kinds of simple bread, the accompaniment to every meal.

FIRST, *KAʿK*,[55] WHICH ARE OF SEVERAL VARIETIES

7.97 **THE FIRST VARIETY** For every 2 kg of flour, take ⅔ kg of sesame oil.[56] If you want to make it with tail fat as well, reduce some of the sesame oil and use fat instead. Rub with the flour until mixed. Pound oak moss, which is called *ushnah*, moisten it with water, wring it out, and pound to the consistency of ointment. If properly moistened, it is easy to pound. Also pound with a little fenugreek and mastic to taste. Then add toasted anise, nigella seed, whole coriander seeds, and hulled sesame seeds to the flour, knead well with milk and sourdough, and leave until well risen. Make into delicate rings. Take the same spices used in the dough, sprinkle some on top, and bake. Have the baker remove them from the oven[57] and top with egg whites, honey, and poppy seeds. Then toast well, and they are ready to eat. If you want them to be yellow, put sieved finely pounded *wars* dye in the milk before kneading. The procedure is the same, and result is appealing.

SECOND VARIETY, CALLED *MUFAKHKHAR*, WHICH IS DELICATE AND CRISP AND MELTS IN THE MOUTH Knead dough with the spices given above and leave to rise fully, then make rings as described. Fill a pan with water, and bring to a full boil. Put the rings on a dowel, stick them in the water, remove, and put on a tray. Do the same with all the dough, then bake in the oven. The result is a delicious and unusual version. 7.98

THIRD VARIETY, A *KAʿK*, WHICH USED TO BE MADE BY AL-ḤĀFIẒIYYAH, MAIDSERVANT OF AL-MALIK AL-ʿĀDIL THE ELDER Take semolina, sprinkle with hot water in the evening without leaving it too wet. In the morning, knead with sweet almond oil and milk, 1 kg of almond oil to every 2 kg of flour. Make into delicate rings and bake. It is tasty. If you want to make all this into molded cookies instead, do so. These will appear in their own chapter.[58] 7.99

THE SECOND KIND, CLAY-OVEN BREAD, WHICH IS OF TWO VARIETIES

THE FIRST VARIETY Take finest white flour and add fenugreek, oak moss, sourdough, and the flavorings described for making *kaʿk*. Knead with milk. Take ⅓ kg of clarified butter for every 2 kg of flour, add to the milk, and knead the bread with it. Punch down well, leave to rise completely, and flatten onto the wall of the clay oven. It turns out nicely. 7.100

THE SECOND VARIETY IS ANOTHER CLAY-OVEN BREAD, MADE WITH DRIED CHEESE Take finest white flour and twenty eggs to every 2 kg of flour, break into the flour and knead with them. Then add the flavorings and knead with milk. The cheese should be *khaysī*, the variety that can be fried, and cut into little pieces 7.101

about the size of a finger. Knead in whole caraway seeds, make flat loaves, and leave to rise. Bake. It comes out nicely.

7.102 **THE THIRD KIND, BRICK-OVEN BREAD RISEN UNDER A BLANKET** This is made the same way, except that when the dough is kneaded with milk, put two layers of blanket on it and leave covered until it has thoroughly risen and become slack. Bake in the oven and set aside. The more you punch this bread down, the better it is and the more crumb it has. Neither eggs nor cheese go into it, except as has been already described.

7.103 **THE FOURTH KIND, A BREAD WHICH THE FRANKS AND ARMENIANS CALL *IFLĀGHŪN*** Take finest white flour. Knead with clarified butter as in kneading *kaʿk*, and allow to rise. Make into a slack cake with a high edge. Take eggs, break into a bowl, and add a little pounded salt, ginger, pepper, peeled sesame, hempseed, anise, toasted caraway and a bit of cumin seed, all whole, and poppy seed. Mix with the eggs, increasing the pepper until you can taste its heat, mixed spices, fresh rue leaf, and pieces of cheese pounded small. Put some finest white flour in the eggs so that they will spread on the cake. Top with a good thick layer of saffron, poppy seed, and pistachios, then bake.

7.104 **ANOTHER VARIETY** It is made the same way in terms of the eggs and dough. Knead the dough stiffly with clarified butter, allow to rise, and roll out a cake. Make a hole in the center with high edges so that the dough stands up and has a border four finger-widths high. Pour the eggs and other ingredients into the hole and bake in the brick oven. It is quite nice. You can also rub its surface with saffron and sprinkle with poppy seed.

7.105 **ANOTHER VARIETY** Knead finest white flour with milk and clarified butter. The standard measure is 2 kg of butter to every ⅔ kg of flour. If you want it to be crumbly, take 2½ kg of butter, knead with milk, add the flavorings, and make into round, thick loaves. Split with a knife into four quarters without cutting all the way through, and bake in the brick oven. Then separate the quarters, toast them again, and rub the surface with honey, eggs, and rose water. This is a tasty dish.

ANOTHER KIND OF BREAD, SUGARED RUSKS Take flour and sugar and knead with clarified butter. If you want it sweeter, add finely pounded sugar. Dilute a little sourdough with a little rose water. Make into rusks of any kind you like. Bake in an iron pan in the oven. When done, remove from the pan, then return to the oven for a second baking. 7.106

REGULAR *KAʿK* AND *KHUSHKANĀNAJ* are too well known to need describing. 7.107

SECTION ON PUDDINGS, OF WHICH THERE ARE TWO VARIETIES

THE FIRST VARIETY Boil milk, and set some aside. Put rice on the rest and keep boiling it until the rice is done and falling apart. Then sprinkle with semolina and cook as a pudding. When firm, moisten with the milk that you set aside and cook as a pudding until it has the consistency for spreading out in dishes. Pour fat, syrup, toasted pistachios, and sugar on top. This is the finest of all puddings. 7.108

THE SECOND VARIETY Cook semolina with water until done and properly thickened. Add fat, pistachios, and sugar, and it is ready to eat. 7.109

SECTION ON RICE PUDDING Boil milk. Set half aside and cook the other half with rice on a very hot fire, so that it boils intensely. Each time it thickens, add a ladle of milk until it is used up, adding ladle by ladle until the pudding is done. It will turn out nicely thick and rich. 7.110

7.111 ***NĪDAT AL-KHULAFĀʾ*** Put 2 kg of bread crumbs through a wheat-flour sieve. Boil 2 kg of sugar and remove the scum. Add 4 kg of honey, after mixing everything with the bread crumbs, moistening with the honey until it is used up. Stir with sesame oil, throw in pistachios, and remove and serve.

Chapter 8

How to Make the Various Types of Sour and Salty Pickles

The first type is turnip pickles

We begin with how to make the distinctive flavoring of the pickles, then how to make them, whether for keeping up to a year or for eating the same day. 8.1

Mustard is the distinctive flavoring of turnip pickles. To prepare, pound white mustard well with a little salt so that it does not become bitter. Toast hazelnuts, leave to cool, rub the nuts until the peel comes off and they turn white, and pound smooth.[59] You can do the same with walnuts.

To pickle white or other turnips to last the whole year, peel, cut into large coarse dice, sprinkle with salt, and leave overnight in a vessel to drip. Remove, put up, and add vinegar and the flavorings. This same method works with other kinds of turnip.

The first kind lasts up to a month Peel the turnips and cut up as described. Bring water to a rolling boil in a brass pan, add the turnips, and remove from the fire. Take the turnips out of the water, put in a sieve, and press with the hand so that the water drains away. While they are still warm, sprinkle with mustard and salt and add vinegar and the same flavorings as above. 8.2

8.3 **THE SECOND KIND IS READY TO EAT IN A FEW DAYS** Peel the turnips, boil until done, and prepare as above. (This is a standard method—it's also how you make eggplant pickles to last a year.) Soak the turnips in salted water overnight, then put in vinegar. The kind made to last a month is merely softened in boiling water; the kind to be eaten the same day is boiled until done, as described in every recipe.

8.4 **THE THIRD KIND IS SWEETENED WHITE TURNIP PICKLES** Peel the turnips and cut in large dice, as big as you like. If you want them to last a year, prepare as described earlier; if for a month, then as we have just described. Sprinkle with salt so that they soften and the juice flows out. Sprinkle with finely pounded mustard, put in a vessel, and cover with wine vinegar sweetened with honey and mixed spices. Add mint and rue, both the leaves and the stems. You can also sweeten with sugar. Some people sprinkle mixed spices and hulled sesame seeds.

8.5 **THE FOURTH KIND IS GREEK TURNIP PICKLES** Take turnips of any size you want. Cut off their stems and leave the taproots just over three finger-widths long, discarding the lateral roots. Do not peel. Make seven or eight slits, lengthwise and crosswise, sprinkle with salt, spray with water, and leave for two days and nights. Remove from the salty water, stuff the cuts with mustard and salt, pour on enough wine vinegar to cover, and leave. They will keep a whole year. These can also be spiced like sweetened turnip pickles.

8.6 **THE FIFTH KIND IS YELLOW TURNIP PICKLES** Cut turnips into pieces any size you want and peel. Pound safflower, make into a paste with vinegar, and color them with it. Pour on vinegar sweetened with honey or sugar and add mint, rue, mixed spices, and hulled sesame seeds. If you like, color them with saffron instead of safflower and pour on vinegar sweetened with either honey, fruit molasses, or sugar along with the inner leaves of mint, rue, mustard, and mixed spices.

THE SIXTH KIND IS SWEET-SOUR TURNIP PICKLES, ALSO CALLED *AL-MUQIRRAH* Soften turnips in salted water, then rinse and sprinkle with mustard. Take black raisins pounded smooth, and strain with wine vinegar several times until nothing is left of the raisins, so that the vinegar becomes syrupy. If it is too sour, sweeten with a little fruit molasses or honey. Add mint, rue, mixed spices, hulled sesame, and toasted hempseeds. When storing the turnips in a vessel, use enough of the liquid to cover them. 8.7

THE SEVENTH KIND IS PERSIAN TURNIP PICKLE Take turnip greens and cut them from the turnip root; leave young plants which have small bulbs as they are. Trim off the withered parts and small leaves and throw them away, and cut the turnip greens four fingerwidths long. Cut the bulbs in four parts, leaving them attached at one end; leave the lateral roots on the taproot. Boil water in a brass pan, put the greens in, and cook until they sink. Lift them from the fire and strain away the water. While the turnips are still hot, sprinkle with salt and mustard, and leave to cool. Take vinegar, olive oil, pounded toasted coriander and caraway seeds, mixed spices, pounded garlic, hulled sesame seeds, and hempseed, and a good amount of hazelnuts, pounded and toasted as has been described. Pour it all on the turnip greens. Transfer to a container and leave a generous amount of olive oil on top. If you want it to last a year, do not boil the leaves. If you want to eat it soon, cook on the fire until done, as described earlier. To sweeten it, add honey or sugar. Put in toasted split walnuts, but be careful not to put in pounded walnuts, which will darken the vinegar. Hazelnuts have a better aroma and do not change the vinegar. 8.8

ANOTHER VERSION OF PERSIAN TURNIPS Put sieved, pounded black raisins in the vinegar; otherwise it is made the same way as the version without raisins. 8.9

A THIRD VERSION OF PERSIAN TURNIPS Made the same way, putting in saffron with more mixed spices and fewer raisins. 8.10

8.11 **A FOURTH VERSION** Thicken honey and vinegar on the fire until the mixture reaches a syrupy consistency. Add mixed spices, hempseed, sesame seeds, hazelnuts, and walnuts—whole, not pounded. Throw the turnip greens in and bring to the boil several times. Set aside without adding raisins. If you wish, add garlic, but it is not necessary.

8.12 **THE EIGHTH KIND IS WHITE TURNIPS PICKLED WITH SOURDOUGH** Knead barley flour with yeast, hot water, and a little salt, then leave to sour. When it is quite sour, strain with hot water in which turnips have been boiled. Set them aside, and dilute and strain the leaven slowly so that it becomes thin and runny. Add thin pieces of peeled turnip, cut from the bottom to the top of the root and boiled in water until a quarter done—the cooking water in which the leaven is to be dissolved. Sprinkle the turnips with mustard and leave to cool, then put them in the leavened broth. Add a lot of mint and rue along with orange petals and mixed spices. Keep the leaven with the turnips in it warm, and in a warm place; then eat.[60]

8.13 **ANOTHER KIND IS TURNIP PICKLED WITH RECONSTITUTED POMEGRANATE JUICE** Pound dried pomegranate seeds and strain with wine vinegar several times, until there is no trace of the seeds. Add honey or sugar and put on the fire until well thickened. Add mint, rue, mixed spices, pepper, ginger, poppy seeds, sesame seeds, hempseed, and toasted walnut halves. When the mixture thickens, chop up peeled garlic with a knife, fry in sesame oil until browned, and add. Then cut peeled turnips into small pieces, soften by salting as we have described, and boil as much as you wish. Add to the pomegranate juice, bring to the boil several times, and put in a vessel.

The second type is eggplant pickles, of which there are several kinds

THE FIRST IS STUFFED EGGPLANT, OF WHICH THERE ARE SEVERAL KINDS

THE FIRST KIND Take celery, mint, and parsley leaves. Select their leaves and some of the stems. Put in a vessel and sprinkle with pounded toasted coriander and caraway seeds, mixed spices, pepper, and whole peeled heads of garlic. Take the eggplants and cut off the tops and some of the sepals, leaving only part of their calyxes. Split the eggplants in four by making two cuts at right angles to each other, leaving the four quarters attached. Stuff the herbs and spices into them.[61] Put them in a vessel and dress with vinegar. 8.14

* **ONE VERSION** is made the same way, but you add saffron to the vinegar, sweeten with honey, and put in a lot of mustard before using. 8.15

A SECOND VERSION is made the same way, but you strain pounded black raisins with the vinegar and use a lot of mixed spice. Then add the eggplants, using enough liquid to cover them. 8.16

A SECOND RECIPE Pound pomegranate seeds with raisins and strain with vinegar. Add honey or sugar and thicken well on the fire. Add mixed spices, mint, rue, ginger, sesame seeds, poppy seeds, and toasted hempseeds. Cut eggplants into thin equal pieces, but not too small. Cut up peeled garlic as well, and fry the eggplants and garlic separately in sesame oil until browned. When done, add to the vinegar and pomegranate mixture, bring to the boil several times, and set aside. This can also be made thick enough to pick up on bread, making for a pleasing and elegant condiment. 8.17

8.18 **A THIRD RECIPE** Cut eggplants into pieces and boil until half done. Then take onions and fry in sesame oil until done but not browned. Take toasted peeled walnuts, pound smooth, dissolve in vinegar along with mixed spices and ginger, add to the eggplants,[62] and bring to the boil several times. Add garlic and transfer to a vessel. Eat when they are ready.

The Third Type Is Salted Lemons

8.19 The first recipe is so well known it need not be described. We flavor them only according to the following recipe, which has two variations.[63]

8.20 **FIRST VARIATION** Take salted lemons, cut up small, put in a vessel, and squeeze the juice of fresh lemons to cover. You can also use sour orange juice, which is milder than lemon juice. Add oil, mixed spices, pounded toasted coriander seeds, minced parsley, mint, and rue, and set aside. It is one of the very best and most fragrant of condiments.

8.21 **SECOND VARIATION** Take wine vinegar, sweeten with honey, and pour olive oil on it. Add the salted lemons whole, and they are ready to eat.

8.22 **THIRD VARIATION** Remove the outer peel of lemons with a sharp knife such that the soft peel does not come away. Rub with dissolved saffron to the most appropriate yellow color and put in a pickling jar. Pour in lemon juice to cover and salt, and seal with olive oil. This variation is rarely made but very good.

8.23 **PRESERVING LEMONS** Many people add honey and a lot of saffron when preserving salted lemons, and it does not turn out well. Here is what we think gives a pleasing result. Take the lemons, split as usual, stuff with coarse salt, press into a bowl, and leave for two nights so that they soften. Press them hard into a glass vessel, squeeze lemon juice and pour on enough to cover, then seal with oil. The brine will thicken well.

The fourth type is quince pickles, of which there are two kinds

THE FIRST KIND If you do not have quinces on hand, take pieces of quince from quince-lemon drink or quince oxymel. Pour a little vinegar on their juice to dilute it. Boil the liquid on the fire and add the quince pieces along with mixed spices and nuts as described above. They take the place of vinegar-pickled quinces, and the result is outstanding. 8.24

THE SECOND KIND Take vinegar and honey or sugar and put on the fire until the mixture comes to the boil several times. Cut up quinces and add, after cleaning them of their fibrous cores. Boil until the quinces are done, and the syrup is properly thickened. Add mixed spices as well as blanched pistachios and almonds, both colored with saffron. Put in a vessel, and it is ready for consumption. 8.25

[SALTED *MARĀKIBĪ* LEMONS] Take large *marākibī* lemons.[64] Cut them in half, retaining both the peel and sour flesh. Press into a bowl and sprinkle with a little salt. Mince a little rue and roll them in it. Cover with olive oil, and they are ready to eat after a few days. You can add a little toasted pounded caraway. 8.26

The fifth type is olive pickles, of which there are several kinds

THE FIRST KIND Take black Palmyra olives and remove their pits. Put in a strainer and smoke from below with Sumatran agarwood and dry walnut hulls. When sufficiently smoked, sprinkle with coriander, pounded garlic, minced parsley, olive oil, crushed toasted walnuts, 8.27

and small pieces of salted lemon. Then knead together. Put in a vessel which has been smoked with agarwood, and it is ready to use.

8.28 **THE SECOND KIND IS GREEN-OLIVE PASTE** Remove the pits from the olives. Pound toasted peeled walnuts and dissolve them with lemon juice, putting in mixed spices, sesame paste, minced parsley, mint, and rue, and salted lemons cut small. Knead with the olives to a consistency that can be picked up on bread. Add coriander seeds, caraway, and a little pepper.

8.29 **THE THIRD VARIATION, LIMED OLIVES,** is so well known it need not be described. The same is true of olive paste (viz., black olive paste).

THE SIXTH TYPE IS CAPER PICKLES, OF WHICH THERE ARE SEVERAL KINDS

8.30 **THE FIRST KIND IS CAPERS IN VINEGAR** Take salted capers and rinse to remove the salt. Steep them in wine vinegar sweetened with sugar or honey. Add a little crushed garlic and pounded toasted coriander and caraway seeds, and dress with olive oil.

8.31 **THE SECOND KIND IS CAPERS WITH SUMAC** Take salted capers and soak them in several changes of water to remove the salt. Take vinegar and lemon juice, and use the liquid to extract juice from pounded sumac berries through a cloth in which they have been tied. Pour the juice on the capers and sprinkle with some finely pounded sumac, garlic, coriander seeds, caraway, and dry thyme. Cut salted lemons small and add. Put olive oil on top.

8.32 **THE THIRD KIND IS CAPERS WITH YOGURT** Steep salted capers in water and rinse to remove their saltiness. Put into either thickened yogurt or dried yogurt, transfer to an appropriate container, and they are ready to eat. When you do eat them, put some olive oil on top. This is a tasty preparation.

THE FOURTH KIND IS MOSUL-STYLE CAPERS Take moldy bread 8.33
and dissolve in fresh goat's milk along with sifted powdered dodder, good salt, and dry wild thyme, all in the fresh milk that has been mentioned.[65]

Or use moldy dough, which is made as follows. Take wheat flour, knead with water, putting in plenty of salt, and form into loaves or thick lumps. Spread bran in a damp place, put the loaves on it, cover with green fig leaves, and put ashes and bran on top of the leaves. Leave for twenty days. When the loaves have turned green and gone to seed, take to a shady place to dry. Pound smooth, put into the milk, and strain to remove any lumps.

Then take fresh capers, remove their leaves and soft, moist stems, and soak in salted water for a day and a night. Remove from the water and pour the milk on them. Add the leaves and stems of fresh wild thyme, a quarter as much as the capers. Put in a large jar in a cold place, and add a lot of salt so that it does not disintegrate; salt is what preserves it. Wash the exterior of the jar with cold water every day. When you want some, add olive oil and the juice of fresh lemons and they are ready to eat. Add garlic if you wish.

ONE OF THE VARIATIONS ON THIS CAPER RECIPE USES THYME 8.34
If you want to put in green garden thyme, use a larger proportion than wild thyme. Put in milk, aged dodder, and moldy barley, then follow the procedure for the capers. This is also a good preparation. There are no capers in it, just thyme.

***PEPPERGRASS** Select stems of peppergrass (also known as 8.35
al-rashād). Put in salted water for three days instead of capers, then flavor as for Mosul-style capers. It is very nice but does not keep long.

The seventh type is bottle-gourd pickles, of which there are two kinds

8.36 **THE FIRST KIND** Take gourds, gently chip off their shells, and split in half. Remove the seeds and cores, cut the gourds into thin slices, and put in a big-bellied urn. Obtain evergreen oak ashes from a blacksmith, sift, and put into the urn, alternating layers of ash and layers of gourd. Pour on water to cover and leave for seven days. Stir three times every day, at the beginning, the middle, and the end of the day. Every time you stir, sprinkle with more ashes. The sign that it is completely done is that if you hold a piece of gourd and press on it, it breaks readily and remains stiff. When the gourd has reached this state, pour water on it, remove the ashes, and wash for three days in water alone until the taste of the ashes has entirely disappeared. Then drain the water and spread the gourd out on a sieve to dry. Take sugar, make syrup, and thicken until the froth disperses and it becomes clean and sticky. When it is sticky, throw the gourd in and thicken the syrup over a low fire until it has the proper consistency. The sign that it is done is that if you take a piece into the sunlight, it looks like amber in translucency and color. If the syrup binds before the gourd is like that, add some water and cook until it does have the translucency and color of amber. Make sure the syrup is thick enough, adding enough white honey to keep it from crystallizing. Add peeled pistachios and walnuts, rose water, and musk.

8.37 **THE SECOND KIND IS MADE EXACTLY THE SAME WAY** Add sharp vinegar, mixed spices, mint, saffron, and poppy seeds, thicken it, and take from the fire. This preparation—I mean the gourd—lasts a whole year. It is a true rarity you will hear about nowhere else. Many people might not recognize it as gourd if they eat it at the end of the year. (The first gourd recipe, being a sweet, was only described here for the sake of this second one.) We learned this elegant and extraordinary gourd recipe from the daughter of the governor of Mārdīn, the wife of al-Malik al-Muʿaẓẓam ibn al-ʿĀdil.

The eighth type is raisin pickles, of which there are several kinds

THE FIRST KIND Pick over raisins to remove the useless ones, wash the rest, and dry in a sieve. Take the smallest ones, wash, and pound in a mortar with mint and wine vinegar; when smooth, strain with vinegar several times until nothing is left of the raisins in the sieve. Take stems of fresh mint and remove the remaining leaves from the stalks. Put with the raisins into a pickling jar, alternating a layer of raisins and a generous layer of fresh mint until the jar is nearly filled. Pour in the vinegar that was strained with the raisins. If too sour, add honey, sugar, or date syrup, according to the disposition of the individual. Add some mixed spices and ginger, set aside, and use after six or seven days. If you want, put in petals of Nisibin roses when they are in season. 8.38

THE SECOND KIND Made the same way, using plain vinegar and sweetened with anything you like—honey, sugar, or date syrup. In this variation there are no pounded raisins in the vinegar. 8.39

THE THIRD KIND IS EARLY-SEASON RAISIN PICKLES Put these into a pickling jar with mint as described and add sweetened wine vinegar, mixed spices, and pistachios. It comes out very nicely indeed. If you want to add turnips to any of these three recipes, cut them in large pieces. You can add pieces of quince and roses too if you wish. The simple version is better. Let every variation stand on its own.[66] 8.40

The ninth type is cucumber pickles, of which there are several kinds

THE FIRST KIND Take October cucumbers, in particular the small ones. Steep in brine for two days and two nights. Then remove from the brine, put into a pickling jar, and cover with sharp wine vinegar. 8.41

Add stems of celery, mint, and rue—more rue than celery. Set aside for several days, and they are ready to eat. They are quite good and last up to a year.

8.42 **THE SECOND KIND IS MADE THE SAME WAY** Add the juice of pounded cucumbers, strained and mixed with the vinegar. Put on the cucumbers with the flavorings, as in the first recipe, and add heads of garlic. It could be made without putting the vinegar in. If tarragon is in season, add some stalks as well. This variation is good but does not keep long.

8.43 **THE THIRD KIND, WHICH IS FULL OF FLAVOR AND APPEALING** Take small cucumbers and cut into round slices. Take fenugreek, soak two days and nights for the bitterness to go away, and put with the cucumbers. Add sour yogurt, which has been drained in a bag until quite thick; add it to the cucumbers and fenugreek. Add stems of mint, and put everything together in a Zabdani pot with a little salt. Leave for two days, and they are ready to eat. This preparation only keeps three or four days. The pot should be new earthenware. Vinegar-pickled cucumbers last a year or more if the vessel is well kept, washed on the outside, and stored in a cold place.

THE TENTH TYPE, GRAPE PICKLES, OF WHICH THERE ARE TWO VARIATIONS

8.44 **FIRST VARIATION** Take bunches of grapes from the Anatolian highlands and seal the ends of the stalks with wax. Pour on sharp wine vinegar and fresh water sweetened with fruit molasses. It will not spoil them because they are similar foods. There is no harm if you leave them in honey, but fruit molasses are better. Know that if you leave the stalk unwaxed, the grapes deteriorate and do not keep.

8.45 **THE SECOND VARIATION, USING LOCAL WHITE GRAPES** is similar, and made the same way as Anatolian-highland grapes.

The eleventh type is pickled green walnuts

In April, take green walnuts which have not yet hardened, such that they can still be cut with a knife. Pierce them in many places with a large needle and soak in salted water for up to twenty days. The water should not turn black but remain sweet. At that point take them out of the water, wash, and dry. Pour on sharp vinegar to which you have added spices and whole garlic. It turns out nicely. You can also add mint and celery leaf. 8.46

The twelfth type is pickled onions, of which there are three variations

THE FIRST VARIATION Take small onions, peel whole, and trim off any clinging peel. Put in a vessel and add vinegar and a little salt. But first soak them in water for twenty days, putting salt and mint on them every ten days and changing the brine every so often until they turn sweet. Then put the vinegar on them as described. Onions pickled this way will keep for a year. Before you eat them, peel again. 8.47

THE SECOND VARIATION, WHICH DOES NOT KEEP LONG Take large Salmani onions, remove their outer peel, and quarter them in such a way that the pieces remain attached. Put water and plenty of salt on them for a day and a night. Take them out of the water and squeeze out the juice. Stuff the area between the quarters with mint stems and leaves, celery and parsley leaves, a little rue, and ground toasted coriander and caraway seeds. Pack in a pickling jar and pour in oil and sharp vinegar. In a few days they will be ready to eat. 8.48

A THIRD VARIATION Cut onions in large pieces and wash in salted water. Pour on vinegar, fresh lemon juice, olive oil, minced parsley, mint, rue, coriander seeds, caraway, and mixed spices. They are ready to eat after one day. 8.49

The thirteenth type, pickled celery

8.50 Take some of the roots, stalks, stems, and tender leaves of celery and put in a vessel. Pour on sweetened vinegar, leave several days, and it is ready to eat.

The fourteenth type, pickled cauliflower

8.51 Take cauliflowers, cut off the base, and pick apart the heads and stems. Put them in a vessel and pour on wine vinegar, sweetened date syrup, mixed spices, rue, and mint.

The fifteenth type is pickled *marākibī* pomelo, known as *sankal mankal*

8.52 I learned this peparation from the domestic servants of al-Malik al-Kāmil. Take large, completely ripe, fully fleshed marākibī pomelos and peel them. Cut the peel into large pieces and fry in sesame oil until done. Then take the flesh and separate each segment; do not touch any of the attached peel. Put them in a vessel and pour on sharp wine vinegar sweetened with honey or sugar. Put a proper amount of peeled toasted hazelnuts, pounded neither finely nor coarsely, into the vinegar along with mixed spices, mint, and the fried pieces of peel; take them from the pan and put directly in the vinegar while still hot. Sweeten the vinegar well; it should not be sour. Leave it several days, and it is ready to eat.

The sixteenth type is pickled roses

8.53 Take Nisibin roses, knead with honey and let them wilt in the sun for several days. Pour on wine vinegar and a little mint, set aside, and it is ready to use. If you do not have roses, take honeyed rose preserves and pour vinegar on them. Increase the sweetness if necessary. It need not be made with vinegared roses; the result is still pleasing but will not keep as long.

The seventeenth type is mock fish paste, known as "village" fish paste

Besides being delicious, it benefits those of a choleric humor and stimulates the digestion. Take sumac, pound with salt, and remove the fruits. Macerate them in a little water, and extract through a cloth so that their characteristic flavor comes out. Leave a little of the sumac without macerating. Then take equal parts minced parsley, mint, and rue, and knead with a little salt in a large bowl so that they wilt. Add toasted peeled walnuts, pounded until they swim in their oil, and a good amount of sesame paste—equal parts sesame paste and walnuts—and fresh lemon juice. Now go back to the sumac juice, pour the ingredients on and mix everything, adding a little of the sumac that was left unmacerated, having pounded it smooth; but do not put too much, or it will darken the mixture. Mix well and add pounded garlic and pounded dry thyme. Make sure to use plenty of thyme, since it's the ingredient whose color and flavor should preponderate. Flavor with pounded toasted coriander and caraway seeds, pepper, ginger, mixed spices, salt, and olive oil. Mix these with the ingredients until the paste is thick enough to pick up on bread. Cut small pieces of salted lemon into it, and it is ready to eat. The more radiant and rosy the color, the better the dish is, and the more walnuts and sesame paste, the more their color appears. When you ladle it out, add plenty of olive oil; do not add spices until there is plenty of oil in the dish. If you like, you can use hazelnuts instead of walnuts and sprinkle pounded toasted pistachios on top. 8.54

The eighteenth type, pickled wild pears, flavored with many ingredients[67]

8.55 Take good wild mountain pears, clean, and cut out the large veins. Cut salted lemons into small pieces and add. Dissolve sesame paste and Baalbek dried yogurt in a little wine vinegar or lemon juice and add, along with toasted walnuts pounded smooth, equal quantities of minced parsley, mint and rue, pounded toasted coriander and caraway seeds, pepper, ginger, rose hips, Chinese cinnamon, mixed spices, a little pounded garlic, and olive oil. The result is very pleasant. Put crushed toasted pistachios on top, or in the dish itself along with the walnuts if you wish.

The nineteenth type is pickled carrots

8.56 Take good fresh carrots, peel, whittle the flesh into small pieces, and throw away the cores. Take honey, wine vinegar, ginger, and mixed spices, and put them on the fire. Bring to the boil several times, add the carrots, and cook on a low fire until the mixture thickens like a sweetmeat. Transfer to a condiment dish. It is tasty. A little saffron and musk can be added.

The twentieth type is pickled fresh fennel, for which there are two variations

8.57 **The first variation** Remove stems of tender green fennel from the leaves and cut into medium-sized pieces. Put in a pickling jar and cover with sharp vinegar. When you put it in the condiment dish, sweeten the vinegar with honey or sugar. This is a very pleasing, tasty and fine preparation.

8.58 **The second variation** Remove tender stems of fresh fennel from the leaves and cut into the smallest pieces you can. Sprinkle with pounded salt and rub hard until they wilt. Leave them in a bowl leaning on its side—a lot of water will drip from them. Leave in salt for a day and a night, and after that squeeze hard. Put in a vessel and add sour yogurt with a little dried yogurt dissolved in it. Mince onions as fine as possible, mix in, and add mint, rue leaves, lettuce roots, tarragon stems, and olive oil. Do not add garlic, as that will ruin it, and in particular, use only the white parts of onions. This is one of the tastiest and finest foods there is.

The twenty-first type is seasoned salt fish, of which there are several kinds

THE FIRST KIND Put a little pickling brine on salt fish along with fresh lemon juice, plenty of olive oil, and thyme. Cut fresh lemon peel along with its flesh, add, and arrange in layers. 8.59

THE SECOND KIND Skin salt fish and cut small. Pour on olive oil, fresh lemon juice, fresh thyme, minced parsley, mint, rue, and a little pounded garlic. Mix and it is ready to eat. This is quite tasty. 8.60

THE THIRD KIND Chop an onion small and fry in olive oil. Add the salt fish whole and fry. Add mixed spices, pepper, and vinegar, and lemon juice and garlic if you want. Allow to cool and it is ready to eat. 8.61

The twenty-second type is seasoned salted birds, of which there are two variations

THE FIRST VARIATION Take the birds and clean them of salt, intestines, and internal organs. Wash in wine vinegar and remove the vinegar three or four times. After that, pour olive oil and fresh lemon juice on them, leaving the birds whole, as they are. 8.62

THE SECOND VARIATION Clean as described and cut into small pieces. Wash several times in vinegar and remove into a receptacle. 8.63

Pour fresh lemon juice, olive oil, parsley, rue, and mixed spices on, and they are ready to eat.

The twenty-third type is seasoned *Iskandarāniyyah* fish paste, of which there are two kinds

8.64 **The first kind** Put in olive oil, fresh lemon juice, hot spices, and garlic, and it is ready to use.

8.65 **The second kind** Add sumac, mixed spices, sesame paste, finely ground walnuts, and hot spices to the fish paste.

The twenty-fourth type is Baghdadi *kāmakh rījāl*

8.66 Take a gourd of 10 kg capacity. Take 3 kg of Persian milk—that is, yogurt—and beat until well mixed. Add 1 ¾ g of salt,[68] put into the gourd, and set in the sun for three days. Then fill with fresh goat's milk and stir with a palm leaf stalk for two days. Take mint, wash, leave to wilt, pick the leaves from the stems, gather the stems, add, and stir. Do not let it bind,[69] but stir every so often; if it binds, the fat and flavor go away. Take an ounce of garlic, peel, and throw in whole cloves. After that, stir twice a day, in the morning and evening, adding fresh milk whenever it decreases. After forty days it is ready to eat. You can put in yogurt instead of fresh milk. The proportions are the same no matter the size of the gourd, so weigh the ingredients accordingly.

The twenty-fifth type is *ṣalṣ*, of which there are several kinds

8.67 **The first kind** Take sour yogurt, strain, and add garlic.

8.68 **The second kind, black *ṣalṣ*** Take crumbs of *kumāj* bread, parch, and leave in vinegar for a while. Then squeeze out and pound smooth in a mortar. Add pepper, ginger, and saffron, sprinkle with vinegar, pound, and strain through a sieve. Cook on the fire until it has a thick consistency, like an electuary.

THE THIRD KIND, WHITE *ṢALṢ* Pound walnuts or almonds smooth in a large mortar. Sprinkle with the juice of *marākibī* lemons and pound, then pour pepper and garlic on them. Add pounded parsley until the mixture thins and takes the consistency of a *ṣalṣ*, and it is ready to eat. 8.69

THE FOURTH KIND, REDDISH BROWN *ṢALṢ* Pound walnuts with a little pepper and garlic until smooth. Moisten with the juice of sumac soaked in a little water[70] and strained through a cloth. Moisten the walnuts until they have the right consistency, and it is ready to use. Add mixed spices and a little mint. 8.70

THE FIFTH KIND, VIOLET *ṢALṢ* Take sour pomegranates, peel, squeeze, and strain. Take walnuts and almonds and pound in a mortar with garlic, pepper, and ginger. Moisten with the pomegranate juice until it gets the consistency of *ṣalṣ*, and it is ready to eat. 8.71

THE SIXTH KIND, GREEN *ṢALṢ* Strip parsley leaves from their stems, put in a mortar and pound until they are like ointment. Add garlic and pepper, moisten with vinegar, and pound a bit until it takes the consistency of *ṣalṣ*, and it is ready to eat. 8.72

THE SEVENTH KIND, OF CHANGED COLOR Pound and squeeze parsley. Take its juice and mix with some juice of fresh or dried lemons, adding the parsley all at once. All the *ṣalṣ* are made this way. Pound walnuts smooth with garlic, pepper, ginger, and mixed spices and moisten with the juices. Pound little by little until it gets the consistency of *ṣalṣ*, and it is ready to eat. 8.73

8.74 **THE EIGHTH KIND** Take one-half part vinegar and one part fresh lemon juice and sweeten with sugar. Add garlic, coriander seeds, caraway, pepper, and mixed spices, using only a little of each so that the mixture does not become too thick. Mince parsley, mint, and rue and throw them in, and it is ready for use. This is the best of the various kinds.

8.75 **THE NINTH KIND, MADE WITH SOUR GRAPE JUICE** Take sour grapes. Pound walnuts or peeled toasted hazelnuts smooth, along with garlic, coriander seeds, pepper, and a little thyme and rue. Moisten gradually with the sour grape juice, pound until it has the consistency of *ṣalṣ*, and it is ready to eat.

8.76 **THE TENTH KIND** Take fresh sour grape juice, add a little pounded salt, and strain. Take the juice and pound walnuts smooth in it. Add garlic and hot spices, and it is ready to use.

8.77 *** THE ELEVENTH KIND, AN EXCELLENT *ṢALṢ*** Use pounded pistachios, pepper, Chinese cinnamon, mixed spices, honey, wine vinegar, lemon juice, mint, and rose hips.

◆

8.78 We begin with the cold dishes[71] each variety of which is made by itself. *Sanbūsak* falls into this category, but it has been described earlier in the book and there is no reason to repeat it.

The Twenty-Sixth Type Is Ridged-Cucumber Dishes, of Which There Are Several Kinds

8.79 **THE FIRST KIND** Peel ridged cucumbers and split into four pieces, then boil, squeeze, and fry in olive or sesame oil. Chop plenty of onions, fry them also in sesame or olive oil, and add minced parsley and fry until wilted. Put all this on the fried ridged cucumbers, pour in vinegar, and bring to the boil several times. Add mixed spices, coriander seeds, mint leaves, and pepper.

THE SECOND KIND Split the ridged cucumbers lengthwise into four pieces and fry in sesame oil. Add dried yogurt mixed with ground mustard, and garlic if you wish, and pour oil on top. You might also fry a bit of onion in oil and put it in, though there is nothing wrong with leaving it out. 8.80

THE THIRD KIND Peel, split, and fry in olive or sesame oil. Fry minced onions and parsley until done and put on the ridged cucumber. Dissolve ground toasted walnuts and a little sesame paste in wine vinegar, add, and bring the mixture to the boil several times. Add some mixed spices and sweeten if you wish. You can also put garlic. 8.81

THE TWENTY-SEVENTH TYPE IS COWPEA DISHES, OF WHICH THERE ARE SEVERAL KINDS

THE FIRST KIND IS PLAIN COWPEAS Take cowpea pods and cut off their ends and the yellow inside. Strip out the seeds. Take water, put ashes in, and leave until clear. Bring to a full boil, throw in the cowpeas, and boil until done. Remove from the water and pour olive oil and finely ground salt on them. If you do not use ashes, the peas will not come out green. For an especially nice green color, throw in a little ground sal ammoniac or a bit of lye tied up in a piece of cloth. 8.82

THE SECOND KIND Pound walnuts smooth until they swim in their oil. Fry, dissolve in olive oil with caraway and coriander seeds, and pour onto the cowpeas. 8.83

THE THIRD KIND Mix lemon juice, olive oil, caraway, and garlic with the pounded walnuts. 8.84

8.85 **THE FOURTH KIND** Take fresh pomegranate juice and pound walnuts smooth in it. Add minced parsley, mint, rue, coriander seeds, caraway, mixed spices, and garlic, and add to boiled cowpeas. Bring to the boil once, allow to cool, and it is ready to eat.

8.86 **THE FIFTH KIND** Instead of pomegranate juice, use the juice of fresh or dried sour grapes.

8.87 **THE SIXTH KIND** Extract sumac berries macerated in water through a cloth and add lemon juice to make it more sour. Thicken with pounded walnuts, pepper, and garlic, and put on the cowpeas.

The Twenty-Seventh Type Is Eggplant Dishes, of Which There Are Several Kinds[72]

8.88 **THE FIRST KIND** Take eggplants, peel them from the calyx end, pierce with a knife, and put in salted water. After a while, put them in a brass pan, and fry in tail fat or sesame oil to cover, tail fat being better and more aromatic. Fry slowly until they are done and resemble marrow. Put in a bowl and sprinkle with coriander seeds.

8.89 **THE SECOND KIND** Fry the eggplants and put sumac juice on them. To make sumac juice, macerate pounded sumac in water, extract the water through a cloth, and add lemon juice to make it more sour. Pound toasted walnuts, spices, and garlic with minced parsley, mint, and rue, and pour onto the fried eggplants.

How to pound walnuts and almonds: Toast them and pound in a mortar, moistening with vinegar or lemon juice, for however long it takes to achieve the consistency of ointment. Sweeten with sugar and they are ready to use.

8.90 **THE THIRD KIND** Fry the eggplants in sesame oil, then take the crumb of cold *kumāj* bread and put it through a sieve. Mince parsley, mint, and rue—predominantly parsley—and rub each herb separately with salt until they wilt. Rub the bread crumbs with them until mixed and add sesame paste and rub until mixed. Then put in mixed spices, coriander seeds, caraway, wine vinegar, lemon juice sweetened with sugar, and a little olive oil. Put the mixture on the eggplants along with a little pounded garlic, which will perfume and enhance flavor.

THE FOURTH KIND IS VILLAGE EGGPLANT Boil eggplants, quarter lengthwise, and squeeze out the juice. Put sour yogurt and garlicky dried yogurt on it, and mustard if you like, and olive oil on top. 8.91

THE FIFTH KIND—BETTER THAN THE FIRST Slice the eggplant and cut into small pieces. Peel small onions, leaving them whole, and put with the eggplants in a brass pan with olive oil, sesame oil, and a little water. Fry over a low fire, shaking the pan, until it is done. Put yogurt mixed with sieved dried yogurt and a little garlic on top, and ladle out. 8.92

THE SIXTH KIND Cut up eggplants small, boil, and squeeze out the liquid. Take sesame oil and fry coarsely chopped onions and boiled eggplant until done. Add parsley, mint, rue, coriander seeds, caraway, mixed spices, garlic, a little olive oil, and wine vinegar. Bring to the boil, and it is ready to use. 8.93

The Twenty-Eighth Type Is Bottle-Gourd Dishes, of Which There Are Several Variations

THE FIRST VARIATION Take a bottle gourd. Whittle gently to remove the rind, cut lengthwise, remove the pith, then cut up small, and boil until done. Remove from hot water, blanch with cold water, and set on a strainer. When the pieces have cooled off, squeeze by hand until the liquid is gone. Take good Baalbek dried yogurt, beat it, put through a sieve, and add mustard. Add to the gourd and mix. Don't use too much dried yogurt. Spread it out in 8.94

a dish, pour on olive oil, and add minced rue. You can also make it with garlic, though mustard is better.

8.95 THE SECOND VARIATION is made the same way, substituting strained yogurt and pounded sugar for the dried yogurt, in which you put the gourd. This variation contains no olive oil or garlic, just mustard and yogurt.

8.96 THE THIRD VARIATION Take gourd, whittle off the peel, and cut in thin slices after removing the pith. Roll the slices in flour as you would pieces of fish and fry in sesame oil. Sprinkle with coriander seeds and put in a bowl.

8.97 THE FOURTH VARIATION Fry the gourd as described above. Add sesame paste dissolved in vinegar or lemon juice along with pounded walnuts, minced parsley, mint, and rue, mixed spices, a little saffron, pounded garlic, and pounded toasted coriander and caraway seeds. Sweeten with sugar, add to the gourd, ladle, and serve.

The twenty-ninth type is turnip dishes, of which there are two variations

8.98 THE FIRST Peel and dice turnips. Take their taproots and the tender part of their leaves, cut three finger-widths long, and boil. Top with olive oil and garlic.

8.99 THE SECOND VARIATION Boil turnips and put pounded toasted walnuts on them along with lemon juice, olive oil, and garlic.

The thirtieth type is fresh fennel dishes, of which there are two variations

8.100 THE FIRST Take fennel stems and the tender part of the leaves. Cut up, boil, and fry with sesame oil and onion. Add wine vinegar and garlic, then bring to the boil. The pieces should be cut four finger-widths long.

THE SECOND VARIATION Made the same way, substituting sour yogurt for vinegar. 8.101

THE THIRTY-FIRST TYPE IS PURSLANE, ALSO CALLED *AL-RIJLAH* AND *AL-ḤAMQĀʾ AL-BAQLAH.* THERE ARE TWO VARIATIONS ON PURSLANE DISHES.

THE FIRST Take purslane, remove the leaves from the stalks and a 8.102
little from the stems, and boil until done. Add sour yogurt, olive oil, and garlic or mustard.

THE SECOND VARIATION Clean as previously described and boil. 8.103
Fry an onion in sesame oil, then fry the purslane in it. Add mint and wine vinegar sweetened with sugar or honey, and set aside.

THE THIRD VARIATION is made the same way, but with recon- 8.104
stituted sour grape juice, lemon juice, or sour pomegranate juice instead of vinegar.

THE THIRTY-SECOND TYPE IS CHARD DISHES, OF WHICH THERE ARE SEVERAL KINDS

THE FIRST Cut the chard in small pieces with the leaves, each 8.105
stalk separately and every piece a finger's width. Boil until done and squeeze out the liquid. Add strained yogurt and garlic.

THE SECOND KIND Boil chard, fry an onion in sesame oil, and 8.106
fry the chard with it. Add sweetened wine vinegar, mint, rue, and mixed spices.

8.107 **THE THIRD KIND** Boil and fry the chard with sesame oil and an onion as described above. Take sumac macerated in water, extract, and strain through a coarse cloth. Pound walnuts smooth, pour the sumac juice on them, and add fresh or reconstituted lemon juice, pepper, garlic, ginger, and mixed spices. Add to the chard and put a lot of olive oil on top, along with minced parsley, mint, and rue.

8.108 **THE FOURTH KIND** Instead of sumac juice, use juice of fresh sour grapes, or if unavailable, then of dried sour grapes.

The thirty-third type is cauliflower dishes, of which there are several kinds

8.109 **THE FIRST KIND** Take heads of cauliflower and boil. When they are done, let them cool down, and split in half. Add olive oil, caraway, ground toasted walnuts, and rue.

8.110 **THE SECOND KIND** Boil cauliflower heads and split in half. Take walnuts, pound smooth until they swim in their oil, and add minced rue, caraway, and crushed toasted pistachios. Take olive oil and a little hot water, dissolve the walnuts, flavorings, and garlic in it, and boil lightly on the fire. Flavor the cauliflower with it and arrange on a plate, putting the flower side up. Pour olive oil on top and sprinkle with pistachios, minced rue, and pounded toasted caraway.

8.111 **THE THIRD KIND** Boil cauliflower and put it in yogurt and garlic. Put olive oil on top and sprinkle with pistachios and rue.

8.112 **THE FOURTH KIND** Boil and add sumac which has been macerated in water, strained through a coarse cloth, and thickened with almonds pounded smooth, mixed spices, pepper, garlic, and minced rue. The sumac juice should be thick.

THE FIFTH KIND Take sesame paste and rub well with rose water until sesame oil comes out, then dissolve the solids in wine vinegar sweetened with honey. Add enough mustard to make it pungent. Fry an onion in sesame oil, add the cauliflower,[73] and sprinkle with minced rue. 8.113

THE SIXTH KIND Boil cauliflower. Take eggs, break into a bowl, and add a little flour, a little olive oil, mixed spices, pounded walnuts, hot spices, and minced rue and parsley. Dip cauliflower pieces in it and fry in sesame or olive oil as you would fish. 8.114

The thirty-fourth type is fava-bean dishes, of which there are several kinds

THE FIRST Shell the beans, and boil. Put yogurt, garlic, and olive oil on them, along with dried thyme. You can use vinegar instead of yogurt, but it does not come out as well. 8.115

THE SECOND KIND Take the beans, boil, and remove their first peel. Dress with oil and dry thyme. 8.116

THE THIRD VARIATION Boil the beans as before and add oil and sharp vinegar. 8.117

The thirty-fifth type is a lettuce dish

Discard the outer leaves, cut up small, and boil until done. Add yogurt and mustard or yogurt and garlic. It is like gourd with yogurt and is made when gourd is out of season. 8.118

The thirty-sixth type is carrot dishes, of which there are two kinds

THE FIRST Cut the carrots crosswise like dinar coins and boil. Put minced parsley, mint, and rue; coriander seeds; and mixed spices 8.119

into sweetened vinegar and pour it on. Fry an onion in sesame oil, add, and bring to the boil once.

8.120 **THE SECOND KIND** Take sesame paste dissolved with sweetened wine vinegar, some walnuts, mustard, minced parsley and mint, and pour onto carrots.[74] The walnuts should be pounded smooth.

THE THIRTY-SEVENTH TYPE IS ASPARAGUS DISHES, OF WHICH THERE ARE TWO KINDS

8.121 **THE FIRST** Choose asparagus tips and cut off their withered ends. Boil and dress with olive oil.

8.122 **THE SECOND KIND** Boil the tips and add sweet almond oil. It is more beneficial for the health and also delicious.

8.123 **THE THIRD KIND** Boil asparagus. Break eggs into a pan with tail fat, keeping the yolks whole. Put the asparagus between and around the eggs. Sprinkle with coriander seeds, leave until the eggs are done, and it is ready to serve.

THE THIRTY-EIGHTH TYPE IS EGG DISHES AND EGG CAKES, OF WHICH THERE ARE SEVERAL KINDS

8.124 **THE FIRST, FRIED HARD-BOILED EGGS** Hard-boil eggs, peel, and fry in olive or sesame oil until the whites are browned. Serve with the cold vegetable dishes.

8.125 **THE SECOND KIND** Take meat, pound, and boil. When done, pound again finely, and fry in fat. Mince parsley and put the meat and parsley in a bowl. Break eggs on top and add hot spices, coriander leaves and coriander seeds, pounded cheese, and Ceylon cinnamon. Fry this mixture in a pan with olive or sesame oil. The pan should be round with a high rim and a long handle like the handle of a ladle. Set on a charcoal fire, spoon in the olive or sesame oil, and wait until the oil is hot, then add the eggs and flavorings—three eggs and a little of the flavorings and fried meat to each egg cake. Fill the pan with the flavored eggs, leave until dried out, and overturn into a bowl. Turn it over and fry the other side for a long time. Prick with a knife and pour on a little olive or sesame oil and spices. Turn over every so often as described until done.

THE THIRD KIND, WITHOUT MEAT Nothing is left out but the meat. 8.126

THE FOURTH KIND IS EGG CAKE WITH FRESH FAVA BEANS OR 8.127
FRESH CHICKPEAS This is made the same way as the egg cake with meat, adding peeled and split fresh beans or chickpeas. Mix everything and fry as described.

THE FIFTH KIND, SOUR EGG CAKE This is made as described 8.128
above, adding finely chopped salted lemons with the flavorings. Fry the egg cake. When done, prod it all over with the knife, spoon on wine vinegar or fresh lemon juice, and wait a little. Then turn over and patiently repeat seven or eight times. It becomes a sour egg cake. Few people can make this well.

THE SIXTH KIND IS EGG CAKE IN GLASS BOTTLES Take the eggs 8.129
and flavorings and put them into glass bottles. Seal the mouths well, set in boiling water, and boil until the eggs are done. When they are done, carefully break the glass away from them and they will retain the shape of the bottle. Fry them in olive or sesame oil. This is put on the *tashāhīr*.

THE THIRTY-NINTH KIND IS FRESH CHICKPEA *KISĀʾ*[75]

Take cooked chickpeas and crush them with a ladle so that none 8.130
remains whole, having set some whole chickpeas aside. Dissolve sesame paste well with sharp wine vinegar and pour it on. Toast

walnuts, pound smooth, dissolve with fresh lemon juice and a little vinegar, then pour onto the crushed chickpeas. Add a generous quantity of minced parsley and mint, enough for the chickpeas to get a good color. Pour on olive oil with mixed spices, coriander seed, caraway, Chinese cinnamon, pepper, and ginger, and mix everything well. Cut in plenty of minced pickled lemon. There should be more lemon juice than vinegar. Put in a bowl and sprinkle with pistachios. You can also put pistachios into the mixture. Put a lot of oil on the surface, sprinkle with minced parsley, and decorate with Chinese cinnamon and rose hips. It should be mixed so thickly that some of it can be cut up on bread when eating. Garnish with a few whole chickpeas. This makes for a very elegant dish.

Chapter 9

On Hand-washing Powders and Perfumed Soaps

Now that we have described the varieties of food, the next step is to describe what preparations are used for washing the hands. 9.1

Perfumed hand-washing powder, seven types in all

The first is Persian *ʿaṣāfīrī* hand-washing powder Pick over 6 kg of washing soda, ⅔ kg of cyperus, the same amount of sieved pounded white oak moss, ½ kg of yellow sandalwood dissolved in rose water, the same amount of ground white rose petals, same of lemongrass, and of clove, ¼ kg of spikenard, the same of Ceylon cinnamon, and ¼ kg of finely ground rice. Mix everything with the washing soda and knead with rose water. Smoke with agarwood for a day and a night,[76] then scent every 2 kg with 2¼ g of camphor. This is a Hammudi hand-washing powder which vizirs and caliphs use. 9.2

The second type is also a Hammudi powder Take 4 kg of the described cleaned washing powder. Mix ½ kg of rice flour with it, and ⅓ kg each of powdered oak moss and cyperus, ⅙ kg each of white rose paste and yellow sandalwood, and ⅙ kg each of Syrian 9.3

oregano and small-leaf basil in dried form. Knead with rose water, along with 2¼ g of best-quality camphor. Spread out in a vessel, smoke with agarwood for a day and a night, dry out, and grind.

9.4 **THE THIRD KIND USED TO BE MADE FOR THE CALIPH AL-MAʾMŪN, MAY GOD SHOWER HIM WITH MERCY** Take 4 kg of the previously described washing soda, 2 kg of the rind of dried common watermelon, 1 kg of pounded sieved sweet almonds, ⅙ kg of ground saffron, and ⅓ kg of clove. Sieve everything, knead,[77] and smoke with agarwood as described earlier. Dry in the shade, sieve, and it is ready to use.

9.5 **THE FOURTH KIND IS A ROYAL ONE, DESCRIBED BY ʿALĪ IBN RABBAN AL-ṬABARĪ IN *THE PARADISE OF WISDOM*** Take 4 kg of washing soda, ⅙ kg each of clove, Ceylon cinnamon, yellow sandalwood, cyperus, storax gum, cubeb pepper, cardamom, and Indian agarwood. Pulverize each of them separately and bolt through a piece of silk. Mix with the washing soda and add ⅓ kg of fava bean flour in place of the rice flour in the previous recipe. Knead with rose water and best-quality camphor and smoke with camphor until it is satisfactory. Then scent 2 kg of it with 4½ g of best-quality camphor.

9.6 **THE FIFTH KIND IS ROYAL, FROM THE BOOK OF MUḤAMMAD IBN AL-ʿABBĀS OF ALEPPO** Washing soda, rice flour, lemongrass, yellow sandalwood, cyperus, and pounded aromatic cherry pits; pound the cherry pits carefully so that they don't oil. Sieve everything, mix, knead with best-quality camphor, and dry. Aḥmad ibn Muḥammad has said that if the cherry pits are pounded in the washing soda and remain in it for a long time, they turn rancid; you must use what you make within a week.

9.7 **THE SIXTH KIND IS A PREPARATION OF IBN AL-ʿABBĀS** One part *ʿaṣāfīrī* washing soda, one part rice flour, one-half part each of nutmeg, clove, and pounded white aromatic cherry pits. Pound everything separately, sift through a piece of silk, and add a little saffron.

Since rice flour has been mentioned, it is necessary to describe how to make it. Take white rice, wash well three times in cold water, then spread it out in the hot sun until partly dried. Pound and strain through a tight sieve.

THE SEVENTH KIND IS A PREPARATION OF IBN AL-ʿABBĀS Take 9.8
equal parts wheat starch, Libyan or Persian washing soda, and white aromatic cherry pits. Mix and put with clove, sweet flag, sweet costus, and nutmeg, these four in the same amount as the washing soda. Scent with ground best-quality camphor.

Section on making perfumed soap

YELLOW PERFUMED SOAP Take a bar of high-quality soap and 9.9
pare it thin until the soap is used up. Sprinkle with rose water and knead like ointment, leaving nothing solid. Pound safflower and *maḥlab* cherry pits and add. Knead the soap with them and leave overnight to ripen. Then spread out on a tray, cut into pieces, and stamp with a wooden stamp. Or put in copper molds, inserting a thin cloth between the soap and the mold, and fill. Leave to dry on a sieve, and stamp, as decoration. When dry, smooth by hand with a little rose water. You don't put safflower in white soap, but white lead instead. Color green soap with a little verdigris, color blue with indigo, rose-red with *maḥlab* and a little vermillion, deep red with a little cinnabar, and pure yellow with saffron. If you wish, put in cardamom, mace, and ground cloves with the rose water. All soaps must contain *maḥlab*.

Chapter 10

On Distilling Waters and Perfuming the Breath

10.1 After washing the hands comes perfuming oneself with waters, which we will now describe. We begin with rose, because it is the favorite. There are several kinds.

The first[78] has three variations.

10.2 **The first variation is fresh red roses which have been watered by rainfall alone** For every 2 kg of petals, take 1½ g of nutmeg, 1½ g of carnation, one *qīrāṭ* (⅕ g) of musk, and ⅒ g of camphor. Grind everything well and sprinkle it on the rose petals, after spraying them with fresh Firuzabadi rose water. After sprinkling the pounded ingredients on the roses, pack the roses into the stillheads, 4 kg to every boiling flask. When ½ kg of rose water has been distilled from 4 kg, pack the still head with roses again and distill. Two grades result, the first with a pungent aroma and the second inferior to it. If you want the liquid to be clear, not cloudy, grind 1⁄20 g of mineral sal ammoniac for every 4 kg of rose water and add. Pour into long-necked glass bottles and seal well.

THE SECOND VARIATION IS A DISTILLATION OF FRESH ROSES, TAKEN FROM *THE BOOK OF PERFUME* COMPILED FOR THE CALIPH AL-MUʿTAṢIM Take fresh red roses and strip the petals, removing the stalks. Pour boiling water on the stalks and cover for a day. Then pack a boiling flask tightly two-thirds full with the petals. On every 2 kg of rose petals, pour ½ kg of the water the stalks were soaked in, then distill. The result is excellent. For an even better result, leave some camphor in it. 10.3

THE THIRD VARIATION Pound well 1 g of musk and 1⁄20 g of camphor in a tub with 1 kg of rose water. Immerse 2 kg of roses which have been watered by rainfall alone. Then pack the roses into a boiling flask and leave without fire overnight to mature. Light a fire under it and distill, but not to the limit; leave some moisture. 10.4

THE FOURTH VARIATION IS BLUE ROSE WATER Pack 4 kg of red rose petals in a boiling flask. Put in 3 g of new-crop deep-blue violets, dried in the sun so that they keep their color, and spray with enough rose water to moisten them. When you put them in the boiling flask and heat it, water as blue as indigo will drip from the condensation tube. It does not stain white clothes. Don't fuss over it while it is distilling, just let it take its course. 10.5

THE FIFTH VARIATION IS DISTILLATION OF RED ROSE WATER Take red or white roses and pack them in the boiling flask. Put ⅓ to ½ kg of vivid red rose petals in the still head and 6 g of the flower called cockscomb, fresh or dry. It will distill a water the color of sappanwood dye which will not discolor clothes. 10.6

THE SIXTH VARIATION IS RED ROSE WATER Pack the still heads with roses along with fresh anemone petals; they will color the water red. It will not stain if sprayed on clothing. 10.7

10.8 **THE SEVENTH VARIATION IS YELLOW** Make it with 1 g of light-threaded saffron. It will drip yellow and not stain white clothes.

10.9 **THE EIGHTH VARIATION IS DISTILLATION OF DRY ROSES** Pick 2 kg of good dried cultivated red roses from their stalks. Soak them with Nisibin rose water for two days and nights in sealed clay pots, then pour on four times as much water by weight. Grind 4½ g of camphor, 9 g of clove, and ⅖ g of musk, and pound well. Mix with the rose water, pack in a boiling flask, and distill. Then pour about 6 kg more water on the dregs and distill. A second distillate will result, not as good as the first.

10.10 **THE NINTH VARIATION IS A ROSE WATER FROM DRY ROSES** Pound 2 kg of cultivated roses picked from their stalks and pour very hot water on them. Cover the vessel's opening and leave for a night, then macerate well. Take Maqasiri sandalwood and mince until nothing is left but very fine fragments. Take ⅙ kg of the sandalwood and pack along with the roses into the boiling flask. Pour the water from the roses on it and distill in the still head. An excellent rose water results.

SECTION ON DISTILLING SAFFRON WATER, OF WHICH THERE ARE TWO VARIATIONS

10.11 **THE FIRST IS REPORTEDLY A MARVELOUS PERFUME** Take ⅓ kg of saffron threads and put them in a glass pot. Pour Firuzabadi rose water on them and seal for a day and a night. Then grind 4½ g each of carnations and Ribahi camphor, mix with the roses, and beat well. Distill with the boiling flask and still head as before. Then pour fresh water on the dregs and distill. A second distillate results, though of lesser quality than the first.

10.12 **THE SECOND VARIATION IS FROM IBN MĀSAWAYH** Grind 2 kg of saffron, pour 4 kg of water on it, and leave for a day and a night. In the morning, beat, stir by hand, knead well, then strain through a fine cloth or some other material you want to dye yellow. Put the water in a boiling flask and distill using the still head. It is also good when distilled with the dregs.

◆

DISTILLATION OF MUSK WITH ROSE WATER Take ½ g of pungent musk and a *raṭl* by Baghdad weight (406 g) of good Nisibin rose water. Grind the musk, beat with the rose water, pour into a boiling flask, and distill with the still head.[79] This is a combination of rose water and musk with nothing else. If you want to add roses or rose water to the boiling flask afterward, you can make another extraction with the scent of musk, though it will be inferior to the first. 10.13

RECIPE FOR CAMPHOR WATER Finely grind 9 g of Ribahi camphor. Then add 1 or 2 *raṭl*s by Baghdad weight (400–800 g) of rose water, and beat well until it turns white. Seal a boiling flask on three sides with sealing clay and examine it closely for cracks. When it is well sealed, set on a burner and pour in the rose water with camphor. Mount the still head on the boiling flask and leave on a very low fire. Take the best part of the distillate; this surpasses every perfume. Afterward you can put in more rose water and distill a camphor water, but it will be inferior to the first. 10.14

RECIPE FOR DISTILLING AGARWOOD Take sound Sumatran agarwood. Pound, grind, soak in 4 kg of Firuzabadi rose water in a glass jar, and leave for two days and nights. Then open the jar and pour all the rose water into a boiling flask with 1⅛ g each of musk and camphor. Add rose water and distill carefully over a gentle fire. 10.15

RECIPE FOR DISTILLING SANDALWOOD Pound ½ kg of finely chipped yellow Maqasiri sandalwood, ground on a quern after being minced, and soak in a glass jar with Fīrūzābādī rose water for two days and nights. Then pour all the sandalwood water into the 10.16

boiling flask, add 1⅛ g of musk and 4½ g of Ribahi camphor, and distill over a gentle fire. If you add 2¼ g of distilled saffron water and 2¼ g of distilled clove water, the result is a remarkable scent.

10.17 **RECIPE FOR DISTILLED SPIKENARD WATER** Take brown *ʿaṣāfīrī* spikenard and select as much as you need of its roots. Pound, knead with rose water and *nammām* water, and allow to mature overnight. In the morning, stir and beat well with rose water and *nammām* water, 4 kg of rose water to every ⅓ kg of spikenard. Pack the boiling flask with it and distill on a gentle fire, but not too long. You can add rose water to the remaining dregs and make another distillation for domestic necessities and hand-washing ingredients.

Recipe for Plain Carnation Water, of which There Are Several Varieties

10.18 **THE FIRST** Take ⅓ kg of carnations for every boiling flask. Soak in 3 kg of willow water, or rose water if you prefer, for two days and nights. Then put the carnations in the boiling flask with the water and distill on a gentle fire until they dry out. If you soaked them with rose water and want to increase the water's pungency and scent, soak ⅙ kg of rose hips in it, grind one *qīrāṭ* (⅕ g) of musk, pound together, add and distill. Boil the dregs with rose water and dry them out; these are used in hand-washing powder, for domestic necessities, and so on.

10.19 **THE SECOND VARIETY** Pound and sieve 90 g of carnations, ⅙ kg of cubeb, 15 g of nutmeg and mace, and 1½ g of Ribahi camphor. Knead with rose water and smoke seven times with agarwood and camphor. Pound with Persian rose water and rainwater then put in the boiling flask. Distill on a gentle fire, without forcing it, to make a water extracted with rose water.

THE THIRD VARIETY Take as many carnations as you want, remove from stalks, and soak in rose water for a day and a night. Distill in the still head on a gentle fire. Their dregs can be used for domestic necessities and in hand-washing powder. 10.20

◆

RECIPE FOR CEYLON CINNAMON WATER Pound and sieve 2 kg of Ceylon cinnamon then pour 6 kg of hot water on it. Leave covered overnight, then leave for three days. Macerate hard, rubbing with your hand, and distill in the still head. If you use half rose water, half plain water, it becomes more pungent and fragrant. 10.21

RECIPE FOR *NAMMĀM* WATER Mince fresh *nammām* leaves and stalks. Put everything in bowls and spray with rose water. Sprinkle pounded agarwood, Maqasiri sandalwood, and ¹⁄₂₀ g of musk on every 2 kg of *nammām*. Add apple peel and citron peel and cover with a lid for a day and a night. Then gather the *nammām* with the powdered aromatics and peels and put in a boiling flask. Pour in rose water beaten with 1⅛ g of camphor and the same amount of ground cloves and distill over a gentle fire. Add an amount of plain water and rose water equal to what is already in the vessel. Do not use extreme heat to force it. 10.22

RECIPE FOR SWEET MARJORAM WATER This is made just like *nammām* water, but with musk instead of camphor. 10.23

RECIPE FOR CITRON-PEEL WATER Rub fresh citron peel with rose water and sprinkle with powdered sieved agarwood and sandalwood kneaded with rose water and smoked with agarwood and ambergris. Perfume with musk and a little civet, then dry the ingredients, grind them to a powder, and sprinkle on the peel. Allow to mature for a day and a night, sprinkle with *nammām* leaves, and allow to mature again. Then pour into the boiling flask with an equal 10.24

quantity of rose water, ¼ g of camphor, and 2¼ g of saffron water, and distill.

10.25 **MANDRAKE WATER** Let mature yellow fruits ripen overnight with fresh rose petals above and below them. Sprinkle with the powdered ingredients described earlier in the section. Spray with rose water, add rose water perfumed with ½ g musk, and distill carefully on a gentle fire.

10.26 **RECIPE FOR MYRTLE EXTRACT** This is used in varieties of *lakhlakhah* incense and as a dye for the beard and hair. When combed in, it lengthens the hair and keeps it from falling out. Strip tender stems of fresh myrtle from their branches, spray with some rose water, and pound fine. Put 4 kg of hot water on every 2 kg and leave overnight. Distill carefully over a gentle fire, then leave in the sun for two weeks.

10.27 **RECIPE FOR ORANGE-BLOSSOM EXTRACT** Distill the orange blossoms on a gentle fire the way you distill roses, and put the water in a glass vessel. Loosely twist a woolen cord and put in the mouth of the jar. Powder some white lead and put into the water and the dissolved blossom water will gather on the cord like an oil.[80] Then put in the sun for two weeks or longer.

10.28 **RECIPE OF PALM-SPATHE EXTRACT** Cut off the outer peel of palm spathe into small pieces. Spray with rose water, distill on a gentle fire, and put in the sun for a while.

10.29 **RECIPE OF WHITE DOG ROSE WATER, WHICH IS BETTER THAN ROSE WATER** This is distilled exactly the same way as palm spathe.

10.30 **RECIPE FOR BASIL-AND-CUCUMBER WATER** Pick fresh basil from its stems and spray with rose water. Cut cucumbers small into the basil, distill together, and store in bottles. When it is sprayed in the steam bath, people will believe that cucumber and basil were available out of season.

RECIPE FOR LITTLE-LEAF LINDEN WATER Take only the yellow flowers, and do not put in any of the bracts, which will make it smell bad. Spray with rose water, pack fresh rose petals in a boiling flask with them, and distill. 10.31

WHITE EGYPTIAN JASMINE water is made like rose water. All distillations are done in flasks on water,[81] not directly touching the fire. 10.32

Section on means for sweetening the breath

A recipe for a tablet which sweetens the breath, whets the appetite for food, and scents clothing—it is made and perfumed with rose water. It can also be ground and sprinkled like an aromatic powder, and is good if you put ben oil in it as if for *ghāliyah* perfume. There are several varieties. 10.33

THE FIRST requires 21 g of Indian agarwood, 12 g each of mace and clove, 9 g of cubeb, 15 g of white cyperus, the same of Maqasiri sandalwood, 9 g of brown cardamom, 1⁄12 kg of musk pastilles, 4½ g of ground Tibetan musk, and 2¼ g of camphor. Grind everything with Firuzabadi rose water, make into tablets the size of chickpeas, and dry in the shade. Put them in the mouth until they dissolve, without chewing, when you rise, after breakfast, or at bedtime. 10.34

ANOTHER VARIETY Use 7 g of agarwood, 1 g of clove, ¾ g of nutmeg, 3⁄10 g of musk, 1 g of *sukk* pastilles, and one *qīrāṭ* (⅕ g) of saffron. Form with ½ g of gum tragacanth melted in Nisibin rose water, knead together, make pills the size of chickpeas, and dry in the shade. You put these in your mouth. 10.35

10.36 **THE THIRD KIND IS USED IN SEVERAL TYPES OF PERFUME** Dissolve it with ben oil and it can serve as *ghāliyah* perfume. Use 3 g of ambergris, 3 g of musk, 3 g of musked *sukk* pastilles, ¾ g of Ribahi camphor, 1½ g of saffron, 3 g of black Indian agarwood, and 3 g of clove. Gather everything. Grind the ambergris with the agarwood, bolt through a piece of silk, add, and knead with Nisibin rose water. Make into pills and dry them in the shade. Use them as described above. Among its virtues, it is a treatment for palpitations—God knows best.

◆

10.37 The book was completed in praise of God the exalted
and by His grace and kindness on the fifteenth
of Muḥarram, 731 (October 29, 1330).

God has perfected the task. Truest praise be to God and
His blessings be upon our master Muḥammad,
his family and his companions, and may
He grant him eternal peace.

Notes

1 Q Isrāʾ 17:70.

2 Q Aʿrāf 7:32.

3 Q Mulk 67:15.

4 Q Aʿrāf 7:157.

5 In some manuscripts six, in others seven, dirhams.

6 That is, pound everything except the camphor.

7 In some MSS, half a *mithqāl*.

8 Sesame.

9 *Fuqqāʿ*; there are recipes for this slightly fermented product in the on-line appendix.

10 Presumably to make into a beverage by mixing with water and straining.

11 An unknown coloring material.

12 See §6.72 below.

13 MS Ṣināʿah 74 explains further: "This is a food you put on puddings, pasta squares, and anything else when you want to dress it up."

14 Logically this step should follow the words "When half done."

15 Sc., and strain the reconstituted juice.

16 Sc., and add them to the broth.

17 *Silq maqṭūʿ*, described at §6.72.

18 That is, giving the usual cooking fat the flavor of chicken fat.

19 Recipe §6.5.

20 That is, along with the meatballs described in the previous recipe.

21 The technique of salting eggplant to remove its bitterness before frying first appears in the tenth-century *Kitāb al-Ṭabīkh* in a dish

called *bādhinjān Būrān*, eggplant of Būrān, referring to the wife of the caliph al-Ma'mūn. Possibly it had been served at Būrān's proverbially lavish wedding. In later centuries meat and other ingredients were added to a category of dishes called *būrāniyyah*, not all made with eggplant.

22 The text is corrupt here.

23 In some manuscripts: do not cover.

24 Stiffer and less delicate than a cornstarch-thickened pudding.

25 §6.33.

26 Or "so that its flavor doesn't overwhelm."

27 Viz. whole wheat boiled with water.

28 Viz. crushed wheat boiled with water.

29 See §5.22.

30 Sense unclear; perhaps related to the following instruction to salt to taste.

31 Ivancic and Lebot, *Genetics and Breeding of Taro*, 60.

32 Three main recipes; five if counting sub-recipes.

33 Viz., plain boiled lentils.

34 Third recipe missing in all manuscripts.

35 Literally, unripe bananas.

36 The recipes do not specify the shape but *sanbūsak*s are generally triangular.

37 This creates a kind of tube.

38 The manuscripts omit the necessary ingredient milk here.

39 A slight variation on *qāhiriyyah*, §7.71 and §7.85.

40 Literally, to the brittle stage, where brittle threads will form between the fingers when they are drawn apart.

41 In Oghuz Turkic, *qarni yaruq* meant "splitbelly," referring to the pastry's shape. In present-day Syria, *kul wa-shkur* still refers to a folded-over pastry, though today it is made with filo dough and stuffed with nuts.

42 Crushed grain soaked with yogurt.

43 Context suggests that it could be used as a *jūdhāb*.

44 Since this is a *jūdhāb*, dispatch to a clay oven.

45 Text apparently corrupt here, perhaps even a fragment of another recipe.

46 Presumably toasted chickpeas.

47 Which was presented earlier as poppy-seed *jūdhāb*, §7.43.

48 *Ḥimmaṣ mujawhar*, literally "bejeweled chickpeas"; presumably for *ḥimmaṣ muḥammaṣ*, "toasted chickpeas."

49 The manuscripts omit the step of spreading the sweetmeat out.

50 Or possibly: "the thinner, the better and more suitable. Roll out *kunāfah* flatbread thinly."

51 If made with starch, this would resemble the Turkish pastry *güllaç*. However, starch cannot be kneaded stiff, so "starch" might be an error for "flour," in which case this instruction describes a crepe batter and the result could resemble the vermicelli-like pastry known as *kunāfah* in modern Syrian Arabic (*kadayıf* in Turkish).

52 *Mirʾāt al-manqūsh*, literally "the mirror of what is daubed"; a utensil used only for making this pastry.

53 The text is corrupt here, suggesting that the mixture must not be stirred, and needs to be translated according to sense.

54 "the shape of an eagle" (*hīʾat ʿuqāb*): the nearly identical recipe that appears in an appendix to Nuruosmaniye 3558 has *q.ṣāb*, perhaps to be read *quṣṣāb*, "twisted tufts of hair."

55 A sort of ring-shaped biscotti.

56 In some manuscripts, clarified butter.

57 This pastry is baked in a baker's clay oven, rather than a home clay oven.

58 The surviving manuscripts of this book no longer have a section on molded cookies, *kulayja*.

59 The recipe omits the step of mixing the mustard with the ground nuts to make it milder.

60 That is, when they are sour enough for your taste.

61 All manuscripts omit the necessary instruction to fry the eggplant.

62 Sc., along with the fried onions.

63 Three actually appear.

64 This recipe of course belongs in the previous section about lemons.

65 This describes making a semi-liquid product with a blue-cheese aroma.

66 A conjectural translation: "Each kind has its own merit."

67 Text corrupt at this point.

68 If a higher proportion of salt is used (the recipe in K. Waṣf calls for nearly four times as much) or the step of letting the yogurt and salt sit together for three days is omitted, the cheese flavor that develops is less sour and rank.

69 That is, keep the mixture well stirred so it does not congeal and stiffen.

70 This refers to reconstituting dried sumac berries.

71 This formula reflects the fact that the cold dishes once constituted a chapter on their own.

72 From this point to the end of the chapter the numbering of the recipes is in error in all manuscripts.

73 Sc., along with the sweetened vinegar.

74 The carrots are presumably cooked in the same way as in the previous recipe.

75 Literally, "garment"; sense uncertain.

76 One manuscript (Ṣināʿah 74) adds: "and smoke with the same amount of ambergris."

77 All manuscripts omit the necessary words "with rose water" here.

78 Indecipherable word, variously written *ḥ-t-t*, *ḥ-?-t*, *ḥ-?-b*, *ḥ-b* and *ḥ-?-?*.

79 Lid and condensation tube of a still.

80 Apparently the lead drives the orange-blossom aromatics out of solution.

81 Boiling water, or perhaps steam.

Glossary

agarwood an expensive incense resembling sandalwood but with a sweeter, more resinous scent, obtained from several species of Aquilaria, particularly *A. malaccensis* (*A. agallocha*). The best quality came from Qamarah, an unidentified place on Java or Sumatra, and the nearby place Qaqullah. Best-quality Qamarah agarwood was known as *ʿud sinn aswad* or *ʿud hindi*.

Aḥmad ibn Muḥammad an authority on perfumery, identity unclear.

Aḥmad ibn Yaʿqūb mawlā walad al-ʿAbbās an authority on perfumery, identity unclear, possibly the "Aḥmad ibn Abī Yaʿqūb mawlā walad al-ʿAbbās" mentioned in *ʿUyūn al-anbāʾ* as an associate of the tenth-century Egyptian court physician Abū ʿAbdallāh Muḥammad ibn Saʿīd al-Tamīmī.

Akhmimiyyah a confection of fried bread, nuts, and honey named for the Egyptian city Akhmim.

Aleppo Ḥalab, city in northern Syria.

ʿAlī ibn Rabban al-Ṭabarī (Abū l-Ḥasan ibn ʿAlī ibn Sahl) (d. 247/861), physician and doctor of medicine, author of the medical encyclopedia *The Paradise of Wisdom* (*Firdaws al-ḥikmah*).

ambergris a sweet-smelling substance produced in the stomachs of whales and used in perfumery. Fresh ambergris (*ʿanbar kham*) has a ranker aroma than aged ambergris. "Triple ambergris" (*ʿanbar muthallath*) was presumably refined in some way. Fatty ambergris (*ʿanbar dasim*) was associated with al-Shihr, a coastal town in southern Yemen.

Anatolia highland area north of Syria, a source of *ʿasimi* grapes.

ʿanbarīnā a compound perfume made of ambergris, musk, agarwood, sandalwood, and the like.

anemone the red flower *Anemone coronaria.*

apple two kinds are mentioned, Hadithi, from the village of al-Ḥadithah, and Fathi, of some uncertain variety or source.

apricot paste (qamar al-dīn) the familiar apricot leather, sun-dried in thin sheets.

ʿaqīd a very dense sugar syrup used to make incense cakes that seem to have the consistency of a brittle candy (cf. Turkish *akide*), so it is presumably boiled to the hard-crack stage (300–310 °F, 148–153 °C). The recipe mentions that it might be boiled even more, which would result in caramel at 320–360 °F, 160–182 °C.

ʿaṣāfīrī spikenard "sparrow" spikenard, the best quality.

ashenkeys (lisan ʿusfur) unripe seed pods of the narrow-leaf ash, *Fraxinus angustifolia.*

Baalbeck Baʿlabakk, village in Lebanon's Bekaa Valley, a source of dried yogurt.

Bardawīl Arabic for Baldwin and the name of four rulers of the thirteenth-century Kingdom of Jerusalem. The rice dish *bardawīlī* is presumably named for one of them.

barmaki referring to the Barmecide family (see Ibn Barmak) as the name of particular varieties of incense of hand-washing powder.

Baysan a town at the junction of the Jezreel (Marj Ibn ʿAmir) and Jordan river valleys, the biblical Bethshean.

ben oil fragrant oil of *Moringa oleifera* seed.

betel aromatic nut of *Areca catechu.*

bizr seeds an ingredient in §1.24, presumably purslane seeds.

black cumin aromatic seeds of *Nigella sativa*, commonly sprinkled on breads before sending to the oven.

black mulberry the blackberry-like tree fruit *Morus nigra.*

bread-crumb stuffing crumbs flavored (*muṭayyab*) with herbs, spices, nuts, and other ingredients, with which roast chicken or whole lamb are stuffed.

brown cardamom *Amomum subulatum*, a spice related to green cardamom but smelling rather of camphor and eucalyptus.

camphor pungent, highly aromatic, waxy substance derived from the wood of the camphor laurel tree, *Cinnamomum camphora*; it was proverbial for its brilliant white color. A high-quality variety was called *kāfūr Ribāḥī*.

carnation the clove-scented flower *Dianthus caryophyllus*.

caul fat a thin sheet of abdominal fat that can be used as a wrapper or sausage casing.

celery *Apium graveolens* var. *secalinum*, the ancestor of modern sweet celery, which was developed in the seventeenth century. Before that time, only celery's aromatic leaves were much used in cookery, the thin, hollow stalks being so bitter they numbed the mouth.

chard food coloring a green coloring obtained from pureed chard leaves.

cinnabar the red mineral mercury sulfide.

cinnamon the variety preferred in this book is Chinese cinnamon or cassia, *Cinnamomum aromaticum*, but some recipes call for Ceylon cinnamon, *C. zeylanicum*. A variety of Chinese cinnamon is referred to as brown and *tuffāḥi*, "apple-like"; sense unknown.

citron *Citrus medica*, the peel was used for its aromatic qualities and the pulp (*ḥummad*) as a sour flavoring.

civet musk of various species of a mammal known as the civet cat, particularly the African species *Civettictis civetta*. §§1.34, 1.35, 1.36 and 1.38 (appendix) metonymically use *zabadah*, the name of the animal, in the sense of its musk, which is properly *zabād*.

cockscomb *Celosia cristata*, a dark red Indian flower used as a food coloring.

cornelian cherry a small, large-seeded fruit with a flavor resembling cherry, plum, and cranberry, *Cornus mas*.

costus aromatic oil obtained from the root of *Saussurea* (or *Aplotaxis*) *lappa*. Apparently "sweet costus" was the mild variety also known as *qusṭ bahr* (sea costus) and "bitter costus" the hotter variety also called "black" or "Indian costus."

couscous in the thirteenth century, the word *kuskusu* could mean either the steamed granules characteristic of North African cuisine or a small soup noodle.

crepes (qaṭā'if) made by kneading a stiff dough and then working in enough water to give it a looser consistency for rolling out, or even looser to make a batter.

crocus bulb (hursunnin) edible bulb of cross-barred crocus, *Crocus cancellatus*. From the name of the dish made with it in MS Ṣināʿah 74 it seems it was colloquially known as *zuʿbub*, "the lowly, insignificant one."

cubeb pepper *Piper cubeba*, a spice of the pepper family.

cyperus (suʿd) the aromatic root of the sedge *Cyperus longus*, used as a spice; in medieval Europe called "galingale," though not related to the southeast Asian spice galangal (*khawlanjan*).

dāniq, dānaq ⅙ dirham; 0.525 grams.

dates *Phoenix dactylifera*, consumed at several stages of ripeness, primarily dry-ripe (*tamr*) and, the sweetest and most desirable form, soft-ripe (*ruṭab*). *Qasb* are described as dry dates that crumble in the mouth. *Qasb* sometimes appears with the adjective *muthmir*, "fruitful," possibly the name of a specific variety.

daʿun an unidentified perfume ingredient.

Dayr Salman a farm town east of Damascus, a source of Salmani onions.

dinar name of a gold coin (Latin *denarius*) weighing 1 3⁄7 dirhams or 4.5 grams.

al-dinnaf sweetmeat made from dense boiled syrup which, in this book (though not in *Kanz al-fawā'id*) is beaten with egg whites.

dirham name of a silver coin (Greek *drachmē*); 3.15 grams.

dodder (ukshuth) a parasitic plant, *Cuscuta epithymum*; it may have been used in cookery as a yellow food coloring.

dried lemons sun-dried, like present-day Omani limes. They could be reconstituted by maceration, as Omani limes are.

dried yogurt (qanbaris) sun-dried and used in the same ways as thickened yogurt. It may have entered commerce as round balls similar to the Central Asian *qurut*, but in recipes it is always used in powdered form.

"eagle" almond (lawz ʿuqabi) possibly a variety with a curved "beak" at the stem end of the shell. It was ground and added to dishes while unripe.

early-harvest raisins (zabib jawzani) made from grapes harvested under the sign of Gemini (*al-Jawza'*), May 22–June 21.

egg cake similar to the Italian frittata or Spanish tortilla.

electuary a medicine designed to be consumed by licking.

elevated agarwood agarwood saturated with thick sugar syrup to add a burnt-sugar aroma to the incense.

fakhitiyyah dish with a purplish color resembling the distinctive throat patch of the wood dove or wood pigeon (*fakhitah*), *Columba palumbus.*

fish paste (sahna') a spiced condiment of dried fish. Faux dried-fish paste was made from ground walnuts and sesame and contained no fish.

fragrant shell *blattes de Byzance*, the aromatic finger-shaped operculum (lid) of certain marine snails, particularly *Strombus lentiginosus*, used in perfumery. The best quality was Qurashi (*azfar qurashiyyah*).

fruit molasses (dibs) sweetener made from boiled-down date, grape, or other juice.

fruit-flavored beer (fuqqaʿ) a grain-based beverage flavored with fruit and spices, fermented for as much as a day but in principle not intoxicating. "Saddlebag fruit beer" (*fuqqaʿ khurjī*) may have been a fruit beer that was fermented or kept in a saddlebag (*khurj*).

ghaliyah a men's hand perfume made from ben oil, ambergris, and musk, often including other aromatics as well.

grain of paradise (harnuwwah) the pepper-like West African spice *Aframomum melegueta.*

green pistachios smaller, sweeter, and darker in color pistachios harvested later in the season.

gum tragacanth (kathīrā') the sap of *Astragalus spp*, used as a thickener.

ḥabbah a grain (of barley), about 0.05 grams.

Ḥadithah a former village in the Ghouta farming district south and east of Damascus, source of Hadithi apples.

Hama city in central Syria.

al-Ḥammūdī an authority on perfumery, identity unclear.

hard candies (aqras limun) made by boiling syrup until its water content is reduced to one percent and it forms smooth, glassy (non-crystalline) drops when dripped onto a work surface. The name means "lemon disks," and lemon juice was often but not always added to forestall crystallization. The candies were often tinted with red, green, or yellow food coloring. In this cookbook, hard candies appear only as a garnish for puddings.

hearts (qulub) nut meats; also stems of herbs such as mint and rue.

hemp seed *Cannabis sativa*; the seed does not have intoxicating properties.

hot spices a loose designation; pepper, caraway, coriander, and Chinese cinnamon are mentioned as examples.

ḥubayshiyyah "the guineafowl dish," perhaps referring to the guineafowl's speckled plumage.

Ibn ʿAbbās (also Ibn al-ʿAbbās) name of one or more authorities on perfumery, likely Muḥammad ibn al-ʿAbbās al-Ḥalabī al-Miskī but possibly Muḥammad ibn al-ʿAbbās Abū l-ʿAbbās al-Khushshakī or Ibrāhīm ibn al-ʿAbbās al-Ṣūlī, each of whom wrote a book on the subject.

Ibn al-Aghlab (Ibrāhīm ibn Aḥmad ibn Muḥammad ibn al-Aghlab, 237–89/852–902), emir of Tunisia.

Ibn Barmak some member of the Barmakid family, which provided viziers to several caliphs and was proverbial for its wealth. The first and most famous of them was Khālid ibn Barmak (90–163/709–80). Three members of the Barmakid family studied alchemy and might have written about perfumery: Yaḥyā ibn Khālid (120–90/738–805), al-Faḍl ibn Yaḥyā (148–93/765–808), and Yaḥyā ibn Abī Bakr (d. 200/815).

Ibn Māsawayh (Yuḥannā ibn Bukhtīshūʿ ibn Māsawayh, 161–243/777–857), physician and author of medical monographs including *On Aromatic Simples* (*Jawāhir al-ṭīb al-mufradah*).

Ibrāhīm ibn al-ʿAbbās al-Ṣūlī (Ibrāhīm ibn al-ʿAbbās ibn Muḥammad ibn Ṣūl, 176–243/792–857), author of various works including a *Book of Perfumery* (*Kitāb al-ʿIṭr*).

iflaghun rich bread with a topping of eggs, cheese, and spices (= Greek *plakous, plakountos*).

al-ʿIraq specifically southern Iraq.

ʿIzz al-Dīn al-Wāsiṭī identity unclear.

jasmine the fragrant flower, either *Jasminum officinale* or *J. sanbac.*

Jew's mallow See *mulūkhiyyah.*

Judge's Morsel (luqam al-qāḍī) a pastry consisting of balls of fried dough dressed with honey or syrup. Unlike the modern version, the recipe in this book is stuffed with nuts.

jūdhāb, jūdhābah a dish consisting of a pudding baked under meat as it finishes roasting in the clay oven. For serving, a piece would be cut for the diner and topped with some of the meat, chopped or shredded.

Jug yogurt (laban al-naʿāʾir) distinguished from "serving dish yogurt" (*laban al-zabādī*), suggesting that it was used in cookery, rather than served as a condiment.

jujube the date-like fruit *Ziziphus jujube.*

Jur Gor or Gur, an early name of Firuzabad, Iran, source of Juri rose petals.

Jurjan Gorgan, a city near the southeastern corner of the Caspian Sea, the ancient Hyrcania.

kaʿk ring-shaped, twice-cooked bread.

kāmakh baghdādī also known as *kāmakh rijāl,* a semisolid cheese.

kashk or kishk crushed grain, often mixed with yogurt and dried.

kashka, kashkāt meat cooked in porridge, more usually called *kashkak.*

kaylajah, pl. kayālij 2.5 liters.

Kerman city in southeastern Iran, source of Karmani cumin.

khaysī cheese a cheese dried until firm enough to be boiled and then fried. From *khays* or *khaysh*, the coarse fabric on which it was dried.

khushkanānaj a cookie flavored with nuts.

Khuzistan southeastern province of Iraq, source of Khuzistani sugar.

al-Kindī (Abū Yūsuf Yaʿqūb ibn Isḥāq al-Ṣabbāḥ al-Kindī, ca. 185–260/801–73), philosopher and scientist, author of *The Chemistry of Perfume and Distillates* (*Kitāb Kīmiyāʾ al-ʿiṭr wal-taṣʿīdāt*), which could be the *Book of Perfumery* (*Kitāb al-ʿIṭr*) cited in *Wuṣlah.*

kulayja a molded cookie with a nut filling.

kumāj a thick flatbread of Turkish origin, cooked in a pan set on embers.

kunāfah a very thin unleavened flatbread of Egyptian origin.

kunāfah mamlūḥah a dish of *kunāfah* cut into noodle-like strips and dressed with syrup. The name looks as if it means "salted *kunāfah*," but as the dish contains no salt (*milḥ*), the sense may be related to *maliḥ*, "pleasing."

ladhan labdanum, an aromatic resin used in perfumery, derived from gum rockrose, *Cistus ladanifera*.

lakhlakhah, *pl. lakhālikh* a compound perfume paste.

"lemon dough" and "apple dough" (khamīrat līmūn, khamīrat tuffāḥ) preparations of some kind which garnish the nut confection *qāwūt* (§7.94).

lemongrass the herb *Cymbopogon* (or *Andropogon*) *schoenanthus*, which has a lemon-like aroma.

linden blossom of the lime or little-leaf linden tree, *Tilia x europea*.

litharge lead monoxide, a red coloring.

long pepper *Piper longum*, hotter but less aromatic than black pepper.

lotus blue lotus, blue water lily, *Nymphaea caerulea*, or perhaps the less aromatic white lotus, *Nymphaea lotus*.

maḥlab seed of the St. Lucie cherry, *Prunus mahaleb*, which has a scent resembling almonds and cherries.

makshufah literally, "uncovered": the sweetened nut mixture used for stuffing pastries when served as a sweetmeat by itself.

al-Malik al-ʿĀdil (Aḥmad ibn Ayyūb Abū Bakr, 540–615/1145–1218), Ayyubid sultan who succeeded his brother Saladin (Ṣalāḥ al-Dīn) as ruler of Egypt and Syria.

al-Malik al-Ashraf (Mūsā Abū l-Fatḥ ibn Aḥmad al-ʿĀdil, d. 635/1237) Ayyubid emir of Harran and later sultan of Damascus; uncle of the author of this book, according to an ascription in the manuscript Ṣināʿah 74.

al-Malik al-Kāmil (Nāṣir al-Dīn Muḥammad al-Kāmil ibn Aḥmad al-ʿĀdil, 576–635/1180–1238), Ayyubid ruler of Egypt and Syria.

al-Malik al-Muʿaẓẓam (ʿĪsā ibn Aḥmad ibn Ayyūb Sharaf al-Dīn, 576–624/1180–1227), Ayyubid sultan of Syria.

al-Malik al-Nāṣir (Yūsuf ibn Muḥammad ibn Ghāzī, 627–59/1230–261), amir of Aleppo, last of the Ayyubid rulers.

mallow common mallow, *Malva neglecta*.

al-Ma'mūn (170–218/786–833), seventh Abbasid caliph.

ma'mūniyyah an enriched rice pudding, named for the caliph al-Ma'mūn (q.v.).

mamzūj, mumtazij literally, "mixed," name of a stew given a sour flavor with sumac and salted lemons; referred to in the heading to Chapter 5, evidently as a shorthand term for sour-flavored stews because no *mamzūj* recipe appears in this book.

mandrake *Mandragora spp*, the sweet aroma of its fruit was said to have sedative powers.

mann two *raṭls*; see below.

Maqasiri sandalwood a yellow variety imported from southern Vietnam.

marākibī lemons some variety of lemon, possibly imported to inland Syria from Lebanon.

marākibī pomelo some variety of pomelo, possibly imported to inland Syria from Lebanon.

marāzibī "princely," referring to the Persian local rulers known as *marzubān*; applied to zinc oxide from some particular source or of a certain grade.

mastic the aromatic dried sap of *Pistacia lentiscus*.

maṣūṣ a recipe for stewing meat with vinegar, saffron, sesame oil, and herbs, originally a treatment for suckling kid.

meat porridge *harīsah*, a dish of grain cooked with meat.

mithqāl 4.5 grams (= *dinar*).

mixed spices a spice mixture which probably varied by time and place. The name *aṭrāf al-ṭīb*, "sides of scent," referred to the paper packets in which the spices were sold in markets. A maximum recipe is spelled out in Chapter 4 but not all the spices listed there were obligatory; the *aṭrāf al-ṭīb* in §2.14 are merely ginger, cardamom, and a bit of clove.

moss, tree moss *Evernia* (or *Pseudevernia*) *furfuracea*, a lichen used in perfumery for its sharp, woody scent.

muʿassalah "honeyed": an unidentified perfume ingredient.

muhallabiyyah a rice pudding named after a seventh-century governor of Khorasan.

Muḥammad ibn al-ʿAbbās Abū l-ʿAbbās al-Khushshakī (fourth/tenth century), author of a *Book of Perfumery* (*Kitāb al-ʿIṭr*).

Muḥammad ibn al-ʿAbbās al-Ḥalabī (Muḥammad or Aḥmad ibn al-ʿAbbās al-Ḥalabī al-Miskī, dates unknown) an authority on perfumery. See Ibn al-ʿAbbās.

mujalladah an unidentified perfume ingredient.

mukardanah a dish of meat boiled until tender, then fried brown, an Arabized form of Middle Persian *gardanag*.

mulūkhiyyah Jew's mallow, leaves of *Corchorus olitorius*. This was also the name of the stew flavored with this ingredient.

mung bean *Vigna radiata*, a small green legume.

muqalla name for dishes that looks as if it should mean "thoroughly fried," but not all involve frying.

muqirrah the name of a certain turnip pickle, perhaps with the sense of "pleasing."

mushabbak a fritter made by dribbling batter into hot oil in a lattice pattern.

musk highly aromatic substance obtained from the scent glands of the musk deer, primarily *Moschus moschiferus*. Tibetan musk, derived from the Tibetan musk deer *Moschus chrysogaster*, was more highly regarded than musk from Chinese or Indian sources.

al-Muʿtaṣim (179–227/796–842), eighth Abbasid caliph.

myrobalan plum-sized medicinal fruits from India of two varieties, emblic (*Terminalia emblic*) and chebule (*T. chebule*).

nadd a compound perfume containing agarwood which could also be burned as an incense.

naduh a compound perfume.

nammām some herb of the mint family, perhaps a true mint such as *Mentha sativa*, perhaps a variety of thyme such as creeping thyme (*Thymus praecox spp. Arcticus*), cone-headed thyme (*T. capitatus*), or common thyme (*T. vulgaris*).

narjisiyyah stew with eggs broken onto its surface to cook there, providing a fanciful resemblance to poet's narcissus, *Narcissus poeticus*, a flower with a yellow center and white petals.

nīdat al-khulafā' "the swaying dessert of the caliphs," a semiliquid sweet.

Nishapur See Ṣābūr.

Nisibin, Nusaybin city in Anatolia, a source of rose water and dried rose petals.

olive oil in this cookbook more often used as a flavoring than as a frying medium. Two high-quality oils are specified, oil of green olives (*zayt unfaq*, Greek *omphakion*), lower in acidity than oil from red-ripe or black-ripe olives, and another oil which may be synonymous, *zayt rikabi.*

oxymel (aqsima) a spiced sweet-sour drink, from the Greek *oxymeles*, "mixture of vinegar and honey." In this book the sour flavor sometimes comes from vinegar or lemon juice, or sometimes from fermentation, and the sweet flavor is provided by sugar, rather than honey.

palm spathe the bract which surrounds the spadices of the date palm until they flower; it has a sweet aroma resembling vanilla.

pasta squares *ṭuṭmāj*, pasta cut into squares rather than strings (*rishta*).

peppergrass, garden cress *Lepidium sativum* (*ḥarafraf, rashād*).

pistachios See *green pistachios.*

pistachio porridge *harīsat al-fistiq*, a rich pistachio pudding fancifully compared to the meat porridge *harīsah.*

pomegranate seeds at most seasons of the year dried rather than fresh; juice can be reconstituted from the dried seeds by maceration in water.

pomelo *Citrus grandis*, a large fruit ancestral to grapefruit, valued for its fragrant peel.

pudding a semisolid sweet. In order of increasing elegance, the varieties were *'asidah*, which might be no more than a sweetened porridge; *khabisah*, containing butter, sugar, and flour, sometimes cornstarch; and *faludhaj*, always thickened with cornstarch.

purslane *Portulaca oleracea.* The leaves and stems were used as a potherb and the small black seeds (*bizr baqlah, bizr rijlah*) as a flavoring for stews and sweets.

Qamarah unidentified place on Sumatra or Java, source of Qamari agarwood.

Qaqullah unidentified place near Qamarah, source of Qaqulli agarwood.

qīrāṭ carat, 1/24 *mithqāl*; 0.19 grams.

qirṭ See table leek.

quince *Cydonia oblonga*. Two varieties are mentioned, *safarjal qaṣabī* and *safarjal barzī*, identities unknown.

qusṭ the volume of either 3 or 6 *raṭls* of water, the small *qusṭ* being roughly 1.2–1.5 liters in Iraq and Egypt, 4.5–6.8 liters in Syria, the large *qusṭ* being twice as large. Note that *qusṭ* is also the name of an aromatic, costus.

raisins See *early-harvest raisins*.

raṭl the pound (= Greek *litron*), a weight of varying value: 406.25 g (Iraq), 450–500 g (Egypt), 1.5–2.28 kg (Aleppo), 1.85 kg (Damascus), 2.062 kg (Hama).

al-Rawandi fried rings of thickened honey, named after the Iranian city Ravand.

red lead also known as minium and lead tetroxide.

red sweet root (ʿirq al-ḥalāwah al-samikhah) an unidentified root used as a red dye for tail fat. *Samikhah* is probably for *samiqah* = Aramaic *samēq* "red."

rhubarb Syrian rhubarb, currant-fruited rhubarb, *Rheum ribes*. The fleshy stalks (petioles) are used for their sour flavor.

Ribahi a premium variety of camphor; the name may be a scribal error for Zabaji, referring to the camphor-producing region Zabaj, thought to be on Sumatra.

ridged cucumber unripe fruit of snake melon (chate melon), *Cucumis melo var. flexuosus*. Botanically a non-sweet melon, it resembles a long, twisty, hairy cucumber with longitudinal ridges and is often marketed as *ghootah* or Armenian cucumber in the United States. This book prefers the name *ʿajūr* in pickle and vegetable dish recipes and the synonym *quththāʾ* in recipes where it is cooked with meat (possibly implying the ripe form of the vegetable).

roll-up (awsat) a pastry, confection or canapé constructed by rolling dough, bread, or a sweetmeat around a filling and cutting crosswise to create smaller pieces.

roses red, yellow, and white varieties are mentioned, and a variety called *nisrin*. That name has been applied to musk rose (*Rosa moschata*), eglantine rose (*R. rubiginosa*) and Damask rose (*R. x damascena*, a hybrid of *R. gallica* and *R. moschata* commonly used for making rose water).

rue the bitter herb *Ruta graveolens*, which has a plum-like aroma.

rumman mukhaththar "thickened pomegranate juice," and the name of a chicken dish flavored with pomegranate juice and sugar, and thickened with ground almonds.

ṣābūniyyah "soapy" sweetmeat, made by boiling syrup with starch, rose water, and sesame oil. It has something of the consistency and resinous luster of soap and was sometimes formed into bars.

Sabur Nishapur, Iran, source of Saburi jasmine oil.

safflower *Carthamus tinctorius*, also known as false saffron, source of a yellow food coloring and also of seeds which could be turned into a milk like almond milk.

saffron the flower *Crocus sativus*, used as a spice and a yellow to red-orange food coloring. "Saffron threads" (*zaʿfarān shiʿr*) specifies best-quality saffron, which consists of the aromatic red stigmas alone with the scentless yellow styles laboriously removed. The styles, called "light-threaded" saffron, were used only as a coloring.

Ṣalkhad a city and district in the Jabal Druze region of southern Syria, probable source of *sarkhadi* cheese.

ṣalṣ, ṣalṣah a class of condiments mostly consisting of ground nuts, a sour liquid, and a spice or herb flavoring, presumably from the Romance word *salsa*. In *Kitāb Waṣf al-aṭʿimah al-muʿtādah*, *ṣalṣah*s are specifically associated with fried fish.

salt unless otherwise specified, sea salt is always implied, the whiter rock salt (*milḥ dharʾanī*) being more expensive. Medieval cookery and medical manuscripts often spell that term *milḥ andaranī*, as if from Andaran, a place near Nishapur, Iran. Nishapur adjoins a salt plain and does produce some salt, though the salt is not particularly renowned.

salt fish in landlocked inland Syria, the only fish used were small salt fish called *sir*.

salted lemons preserved by salting, valued for their aromatic peel.

sanbusak, sanbusaj a pastry made folding dough over a filling (usually savory but sometimes sweet) into a triangle and frying it; the Indian samosa is descended from the same medieval Persian ancestor.

sandarac resin of the Moroccan tree *Tetraclinis articulate*, an incense with a balsam-like aroma.

sappanwood a red dye obtained from the Indonesian tree *Caesalpinia sappan*, related to the New World tree brazilwood (*C. echinata*).

sarkhadi cheese a hard cheese that could be slivered like carrots.

semolina a variety of hard wheat, *Triticum durum*; the word also refers to the texture of meal, ground coarser than flour but finer than grits.

sesame *Sesamum indicum*. The oil (*shīraj*) served primarily for frying, particularly for pastries. Toasted sesame oil (*ḥuraqat al-shīraj*) was used sparingly as a flavoring. Sesame paste is also known as tahini.

Shayzariyyah a sweetmeat named for the Syrian city Shayzar.

shishsh a sort of near beer flavored with orange peel and spices.

sikanjubin a beverage of honey mixed with vinegar, closer to the original Greek recipe of oxymel than *aqsima*.

sikbaj meat stewed with vinegar, saffron, and fruits and vegetables of choice; to judge by the subsequent history of the name in Europe (*escabeche*, aspic), it was served cold as a tart, jellied dish.

sitt al-shunaʿ a stew containing taro.

sour cherry *Prunus cerasus*. Note that the word *qarāṣiyā* has also referred to a small dark plum.

sour grape (ḥiṣrim) either a particular strain of *Vitis vinifera* with naturally sour juice or ordinary wine grapes picked unripe. The dried form (*ḥiṣrim ʿatīq*) could be reconstituted by maceration.

sour orange Seville orange, *Citrus x aurantium*, valued for its peel and sour juice.

soy sauce salty liquid seasoning made in the medieval Arab world from bread or barley dough cultured with molds of the genus *Aspergillus*, rather than from soy beans as in the Far East. It was popular in medieval Iraq and North Africa but less so in Syria; unlike several other medieval books, *Wuṣlah* does not give a recipe for it and only calls for it once, in §6.47. The mold-cultured grain (*qamnah* = Syriac *qamlā* "bread mold") is added to milk in §8.34 to give a blue-cheese flavor, because it also contained *Penicillium* molds.

spikenard See *ʿaṣāfīrī spikenard.*

starch the medieval product was extracted from a stiff dough by kneading it under water. Unlike modern cornstarch, it contained some gluten. It was used as the fresh liquid suspension (*malban*) or in dried form (*nisha'*), either ground or in sheets.

stinking ground pine *Camphorosma monspeliaca,* a low-growing plant which smells of camphor.

storax aromatic gum of Turkish sweetgum, *Liquidambar orientalis.*

stuffed eggplants and ridged cucumber are stuffed in §6.32, §§6.35–39 and §§8.14–16. Early on the word *maḥshī* ("stuffed") became confused with *maḥsī* ("soupy"), a preparation with the consistency of modern dips such as baba ghannouj. §§8.17–18, although in the *maḥshī* section, are actually such dips.

stuffed pasta (*shushbarak)* a ravioli-like stuffed pasta resembling the Italian cappelletti, made by folding a circle of paste over a meat filling and then folding the "arms" over each other. This book does not give a *shushbarak* recipe and mentions it only in the *nāṣiriyyah* recipe, §7.14, in connection with the mold used for shaping it.

subiyyah a frothy near-beer flavored with spices and incense.

sugar it appeared in several degrees of refinement: rock candy (*sukkar nabat*), brown sugar (*sukkar sulaymani*), white sugar (*sukkar abyaḍ*), and finest white sugar (*sukkar ṭabarzad*), refined by boiling crude syrup with milk to precipitate impurities.

sugar syrup see *syrup.*

sukk a perfume and incense made from ground oak galls kneaded with water, rubbed with jasmine oil, mixed with musk, and formed into disks which would be pierced and dried on a string. A richer version, *sukk al-misk,* was made with 2 ¼ g of musk to the kilogram.

sumac dried fruits of tanner's sumac, *Rhus coriaria,* used as a spice and a sour flavoring. The plant bears its fruits in dense clusters known as sumac bobs. Because they are purplish red and are borne pointing upward, this book refers to them as sumac "flowers" (*zahr summaq*). The actual flowers of the sumac plant have no aroma.

sweet flag *Acorus calamus*; the leaves are aromatic and the rhizome has been used as a substitute for sweet spices such as ginger and nutmeg.

sweet-kerneled apricot an apricot variety with almond-like edible seeds.

Syrian oregano *Origanum syriacum*, an ingredient evidently unfamiliar to the scribes. *Marmākhūz* is the spelling that appears in Topkapı, other manuscripts have *marmahur*, *marmajur*, and *sarmahur*.

syrup this book distinguishes the following densities of sugar syrup. "Syrup" without a further qualification in the text might refer to any of the first five stages below:

1. thin syrup, probably equal quantities of sugar and water;
2. strong syrup, made with twice as much sugar as water;
3. sticky syrup, boiled until its foam disperses and it becomes clear and sticky, likely the stages known as small to large gloss (214–217 °F, 101.1–102.8 °C);
4. thick or properly thickened syrup, suitable for dressing pastries, presumably boiled to the small pearl stage (220 °F, 104.4 °C);
5. thread stage syrup, boiled until brittle threads will form between the fingers when separated (about 225 °F, 107 °C) and used in the same ways as "properly thickened" syrup, but perhaps a little denser;
6. syrup which will form a long thread ("hair") when poured from a spoon, the soft ball stage (about 235 °F, 113 °C);
7. chewy syrup, the hard ball to soft crack stage (250–290 °F, 121–143.3 °C), at which syrup will form a sheet resembling an almond leaf when dripped from a utensil pierced with a number of holes;
8. powerfully thickened syrup contained honey, which can prevent crystallization, suggesting the soft crack stage (270–290 °F, 132–143 °C);
9. cracking and shattering syrup, the hard crack stage (300–310 °F, 148–153 °F);
10. scalded, or perhaps burnt, syrup, presumably caramel (320–360 °F, 160–182 °C).

tabbālah a disk of meat and a starch on which savory foods and snacks such as roast meat or *sanbusak* were presented.

table leek *qirṭ*, a mild leek, perhaps the same as *tarreh*, the variety of *Allium ampeloprasum* known as Persian leek or Persian chives (= Aramaic *qarta* "leek").

tail fat tail and rump of Middle Eastern sheep, in which the animal's subcutaneous fat is concentrated; with a lower melting point than internal fat it is palatable for cooking.

ṭarāṭir al-Turkumān the tall hats of the Turkish nomads.

taro root *Colocasia esculenta*, used in similar ways to potato.

tashāhīr literally, "acts of exposing." The precise meaning of the word in cookery is unclear but they seem to have been edible things on which small cooked savory items were presented. In Chapter 5, for instance, boiled eggs are served on *tashāhīr* or square pasta, ravioli, cold vegetable dishes, or meat pastries (*sanbūsak*).

thickened yogurt yogurt drained of whey.

thyme common thyme, *Thymus vulgaris*, possibly cone-headed thyme, *T. capitatus*.

truffle the desert truffle, *Terfezia spp.*

ūqiyah the ounce (=Latin *uncia*), 1⁄12 *raṭl* to 33.85 g (Iraq), 37.5–41.67 g (Egypt), 125 g–190 g (Aleppo), 154.17 g (Damascus), 171.83 g (Hama).

uropygium the fatty, fleshy protuberance of a bird's rear that bears the tail feathers, colloquially known as the parson's nose or Pope's nose.

ushnan perfumed powder used after eating to cleanse the hands.

verdigris the green compound copper acetate.

vermillion a scarlet coloring made from cinnabar.

wars a yellow dye obtained from *Flemingia grahamiana (rhodocarpa)*.

white lead a white coloring also known as ceruse, basic lead carbonate.

wild pear *Pyrus syriaca* Boiss., a small roundish pear, edible when very ripe but containing hard lumps.

willow the leaves were distilled to make an aromatic water and the twigs were made into toothpicks.

al-Zabdani (or al-Zabadani) a hill town northwest of Damascus, producer of pots.

zīrabāj a particular thickened sweet-sour stew made with nuts and/or fruits.

zulabiyyah, zulabiya a fritter; in the tenth century it was sheets of dough rolled out and then fried, later more usually made by dribbling batter into hot oil. See *mushabbak.*

Weights and Measures

dāniq	⅙ *dirham*; 0.525 g
dirham	name of a silver coin (Greek *drachmē*); 3.15 g
dīnār	name of a gold coin (Latin *denarius*) weighing 1 3/7 dirhams; 4.5 g
grain	(of barley; *ḥabbah*), about 0.05 g
kaylajah	2.5 liters
mann	two *raṭl*s; see below
mithqāl	4.5 g (= *dīnār*)
qīrāṭ	carat, 0.2 g
raṭl	a weight of varying value: 406.25 g (Iraq), 450–500 g (Egypt), 1.5–2.28 kg (Aleppo), 1.85 kg (Damascus), 2.062 kg (Hama)
ūqiyah	1/12 *raṭl*: 33.85 g (Iraq), 37.5–41.67 g (Egypt), 125–190 g (Aleppo), 154.17 g (Damascus), 171.83 g (Hama)

Bibliography

Al-Baghdādī (al-Kātib), Muḥammad ibn al-Ḥasan ibn Muḥammad ibn al-Karīm. *Kitāb al-Ṭabīkh*. Translated by Charles Perry. Totnes, Devon: Prospect Books, 2004. Turkish translation (of the English): Nazlı Piskin, *Kitâbü't-Tabih*. Istanbul: Kitapyayınevi, 2009. Prospect Books, 2000. Ottoman translation: Şirvani, Muhammad bin Mahmud. *Tercüme-i Kitâbü't-Tabih*. Ali Emiri Mütaferrik 143, Millet Kütüphanesi, Istanbul. Şirvani translated by Mustafa Argunşah and Müjgân Çakır as *15. Yüzyıl Osmanlı Mutfağı*. Istanbul: Gökkubbe Yayınları, 2005.

Barreveld, W. H. *Date Palm Products*. FAO Agricultural Services Bulletin #101. Rome: Food and Agricultural Organization of the United Nations, 1993.

Chipman, Leigh. *The World of Pharmacy and Pharmacists in Mamluk Cairo*. Leiden: Brill, 2009.

Escoffier, Auguste. *The Escoffier Cookbook* (translation of *Le Guide Culinaire*). New York: Crown, 1969.

Facciola, Stephen. *Cornucopia II: A Source Book of Edible Plants*. Vista, California: Kampong Publications, 1998.

Hinz, Walther. *Islamische Masse und Gewichte*. Leiden: E. J. Brill, 1958.

Ibn al-ʿAdīm. *Kitāb al-Wuṣlah ilā l-ḥabīb fī waṣf al-ṭayyibāt wal-ṭīb*. Edited by Sulaymā Maḥjūb and Durriyyah al-Khaṭīb. Aleppo: University of Aleppo, 1988.

Ibn Naṣr ibn Sayyār, Abū Muḥammad al-Muẓaffar. *Kitāb al-Ṭabīkh*. Edited by Kai Öhrnberg and Sahban Mroueh. Helsinki: Finnish Oriental Society, 1987. Translated by Nawal Nasrallah as *Annals of the Caliphs'*

Kitchens: Ibn Sayyār al-Warrāq's Tenth-Century Baghdadi Cookbook. Leiden: Brill, 2007.

Lebot, Vincent and Anton Ivancic. *The Genetics and Breeding of Taro.* Versailles: Editions Quae, 2000.

Lev, Efraim and Zohar Amar. *Practical* Materia Medica *of the Medieval Eastern Mediterranean According to the Cairo Genizah.* Leiden and Boston: Brill, 2008.

Marin, Manuela and David Waines, eds. *Kanz al-fawā'id fī tanwī' al-mawā'id.* Wiesbaden: Franz Steiner Verlag, 1993.

Martellotti, Anna. *Il Liber de Ferculis di Giambonino da Cremona.* Faisano, Bari: Schena, 2002.

Al-Mas'ūdī, 'Alī ibn al-Ḥusayn. *Murūj al-dhahab.* Edited by Barbier de Meynard and Pavet de Courteille, revised by Charles Pellat, 7 vols. Beirut: Université Libanaise, 1966–74.

McGee, Harold. *On Food and Cooking: The Science and Lore of the Kitchen.* New York: Scribner, 2004.

Perry, Charles, trans. "*Kitāb Waṣf al-aṭ'imah al-mu'tādah*" ("The Description of Familiar Foods," Topkapi 62 Tip 1992 and 22/74 Tip 2004). In *Medieval Arab Cookery,* essays and translations by Maxime Rodinson, A.J. Arberry, and Charles Perry, 273–465. Totnes, Devon: Prospect Books, 2001.

Rodinson, Maxime. "Études sur manuscrits Arabes relatifs à la cuisine." *Révue des Études Islamiques,* 1948. Translated by Barbara Inskip as "Studies in Arabic Manuscripts Relating to Cookery." In *Medieval Arab Cookery,* 91–163. Totnes, Devon: Prospect Books, 2000.

Wissa Wassef, Cérès. *Pratiques rituelles et alimentaires des coptes.* Cairo: Institute Français d'Archéologie Orientale du Caire, 1971.

Index

pepper, long, §4.4, §6.23
peppergrass, §8.35
pistachios, xxxi, xl, xli; in bread, §7.97, §7.103; in bread-crumb stuffing, §§5.6–10, §5.15; in chicken dishes, §5.2, §§5.6–10, §5.15, §5.17, §§5.22–23, §5.25, §5.28, §5.33, §§5.45–46, §5.49, §5.58, §5.60, §5.65, §§5.67–68, §5.70, §5.74, §5.76; chicken with plain pistachio stuffing, §5.25; in crepes, §§7.25–30; in *kunāfah mamlūḥah*, §§7.20–23; in lamb dishes, §6.3, §6.5, §6.20, §6.41, §6.44, §6.52, §6.89, §§6.92–94, §6.98, §§6.104–5, §6.106, §6.117, §6.121, §6.132, §§6.137–38; in lamb with banana dishes, §§6.137–38; in *ma'mūniyyah*, §§7.5–7; in pickles and cold dishes, §8.25, §8.36, §8.40, §8.54, §8.55, §8.77, §8.110, §8.130; pistachio chicken, §5.60; pistachio porridge (*harīsat al-fistiq*), §4.3, §§7.8–10, §7.75; in pudding, xli, §7.6, §7.48, §§7.108–9; in rice dishes, §5.74, §6.89, §§6.92–94, §6.98; in *sanbūsak*, §6.3, §6.5; in sweets and baked goods, §7.1, §7.3, §§7.5–7, §§7.8–10, §§7.11–14, §7.18, §§7.20–23, §§7.25–30, §7.34, §7.36, §7.42, §7.45, §§7.48–49, §§7.53–95 passim, §7.97, §7.103, §§7.108–9, §7.111; in *zīrbāj*, §§6.104–5
pistachios, green, §5.33, §6.52, §6.92
pomegranate, xxx, xxxi, xxxvii; in beverages, §2.5, §2.7, §2.9, §2.11; in chicken dishes, §5.16, §§5.34–37, §5.40, §5.70; chicken with pomegranate juice, §§5.34–37; in lamb dishes, §6.96; in perfumes, §§1.15–16; in pickles and cold dishes, §8.13, §8.17, §8.71, §8.85, §8.104; in sweets and baked goods, §7.6
pomelo, §1.14, §2.13; *marākibī* pomelo, §8.52
poppy seed: in lamb dishes, §6.5, §6.44; poppy-seed chicken, §5.63; poppy-seed *jūdhāb*, §7.43; in pickles, §8.13, §8.17, §8.37; in sweets and baked goods, §7.43, §7.45, §7.51, §7.53, §7.55, §7.56, §7.57, §7.58, §7.72, §7.87, §7.92, §§7.103–4
psyllium, §1.13, §1.24, §1.28
purslane, §6.70, §§8.102–4
purslane seeds (*bizr baqlah*), §5.64, §7.55

qāhiriyyah, §7.71, §7.85, 144n39
Qamarah (Qamari agarwood), §1.14, §1.21, §1.23, §1.24
qanbarīs. *See* yogurt, dried
Qaqullah (Qaqulli agarwood), §1.13, §2.15
qarāṣiyā. *See* cherries (sour)
qāwūt, §7.94
qīrāṭ, §10.2, §10.9, §10.18, §§10.24–25, §10.35
qirṭ. *See* table leek
Queen of Nubia (*sitt al-nūbah*), §5.64
quern, §1.29, §10.16
quince, xl; in beverages, §2.11, §2.15; in chicken dishes, §5.23, §5.36, §§5.45–48; chicken with quince, §§5.45–48; in lamb dishes, §6.9, §6.80, §§6.104–5, §§6.117–18; in perfumes, §1.12,

chicken, §5.66; rose water, distillation of, §§10.1–10; in sweets and baked goods, §7.59. *See also* rose water
rue, xxxvii; in beverages, §§2.1–3, §§2.5–6, §§2.13–14; in bread, §7.103; in bread-crumb stuffing, §§5.6–15; in cauliflower dishes, §8.51, §§8.109–14; in chicken dishes, §§5.6–15, §§5.22–24, §5.76; in eggplant dishes, §6.34, §8.17, §§8.89–90, §8.93; in fruit juice, §3.4; in lamb dishes, §6.2, §6.20, §6.34, §6.80, §§6.106–7, §§6.111–13; in pickles and cold dishes, §8.4, §§8.6–7, §§8.12–13, §8.17, §8.20, §8.26, §8.28, §8.41, §§8.48–49, §8.51, §8.54, §8.55, §8.58, §8.60, §8.63, §§8.74–75, §8.85, §§8.89–90, §8.93, §8.94, §8.97, §§8.106–7, §§8.109–14, §8.119; in turnip pickles, §8.4, §§8.6–7, §§8.12–13
rummān mukhaththar, §5.36

ṣābūniyyah, §7.13, §§7.14–15, §7.52, §7.58, §7.60, §7.75
saddlebag fruit beer, §2.1, §2.3, 143n9
safflower, §5.31, §§6.114–15, §8.6, §9.9
saffron: in chicken dishes, §5.4, §5.16, §5.17, §5.20, §5.22, §5.28, §5.45, §5.48, §5.49, §5.62, §5.65, §5.68; in fragrant waters, distillation of, §10.8, §§10.11–12, §10.16, §10.24, §10.35, §10.36; in hand-washing powders, §9.4, §9.7; in lamb dishes, §6.5, §6.12, §6.17, §§6.43–44, §§6.65–66, §6.76, §6.89, §§6.93–94, §6.104, §6.109, §6.111, §6.117, §6.121, §6.125, §6.133, §6.138; in perfumes, §§1.7–8, §§1.10–11, §§1.13–17, §1.24, §§1.27–28; in pickles and cold dishes, §8.6, §8.10, §8.15, §§8.22–23, §8.25, §8.37, §8.56, §8.68, §8.97; in soap, §9.9; in sweets and baked goods, §7.4, §7.37, §7.38, §§7.42–45, §7.53, §§7.57–58, §§7.72–73, §7.87, §§7.90–91, §7.94, §§7.103–4; saffron water, distillation of, §§10.11–12
ṣaḥnā'. *See* fish paste
sal ammoniac, §8.82, §10.2
Ṣalkhad. *See ṣarkhadī* cheese
ṣalṣ, xlii, §§8.67–77
sanbūsak, xxviii, xlii, §5.21, §§6.2–5, §6.22, §6.85, §6.128, §6.129, §7.1, §7.63, §7.80, §8.78, 144n36
sandalwood, xxxiv, xxxix; in breath fresheners, §10.34; distillation of, §10.16; in fragrant waters, distillation of, §10.10, §10.16, §10.22, §10.24; in hand-washing powders, §§9.2–3, §§9.5–6; Maqasiri, §§1.2–3, §1.10, §§1.13–16, §§1.20–21, §1.23, §1.27, §§1.30–32, §10.10, §10.16, §10.22, §10.34; in perfumes, §§1.2–3, §1.10, §§1.13–16, §§1.20–24, §§1.27–28, §§1.30–32
sandarac, §1.28
sappanwood, §10.6
ṣarkhadī cheese, §6.61
sausage casing (*sakhtūr*, pl. *sakhātīr*), §5.18
semolina, §7.36, §7.40, §§7.43–44, §7.46, §§7.78–79, §7.91, §7.94, §7.99, §§7.108–9
sesame paste (tahini), xxxi, xxxvi; in chicken dishes, §5.8, §5.15, §6.21;

§8.102, §8.105, §8.111, §8.115, §8.118, 146n68; thickened yogurt, §8.32. *See also* yogurt, dried
yogurt, dried (*qanbarīs*): in chicken with lemon, §5.31; in eggplant dishes, §6.29, §§8.91–92; in lamb dishes, §6.29, §6.36, §6.46, §6.60, §6.102; in pickles and cold dishes, §8.32, §8.55, §8.58, §8.80, §§8.91–92, §8.93, §§8.94–95

al-Zabdānī (Zabdani pots), §8.43
Zaynab's Fingers, §7.65
zinc oxide, §1.25
zīrabāj, §§5.49–51
zulābiyyah, §7.11

About the NYU Abu Dhabi Institute

The Library of Arabic Literature is supported by a grant from the NYU Abu Dhabi Institute, a major hub of intellectual and creative activity and advanced research. The Institute hosts academic conferences, workshops, lectures, film series, performances, and other public programs directed both to audiences within the UAE and to the worldwide academic and research community. It is a center of the scholarly community for Abu Dhabi, bringing together faculty and researchers from institutions of higher learning throughout the region.

NYU Abu Dhabi, through the NYU Abu Dhabi Institute, is a world-class center of cutting-edge research, scholarship, and cultural activity. The Institute creates singular opportunities for leading researchers from across the arts, humanities, social sciences, sciences, engineering, and the professions to carry out creative scholarship and conduct research on issues of major disciplinary, multidisciplinary, and global significance.

About the Translator

Charles Perry majored in Middle East Studies at Princeton University and the University of California, Berkeley, and earned the British Foreign Office's Advanced Interpretership Certificate at the Middle East Centre for Arab Studies, Shimlan, Lebanon. After university he chose a journalistic career, beginning at *Rolling Stone Magazine* in 1968 and culminating in eighteen years as a staff writer for the *Los Angeles Times* food section. He has published widely on the history of Middle Eastern food, including a translation of *A Baghdad Cookery Book: The Book of Dishes*, by Muḥammad ibn al-Ḥasan al-Baghdādī.

The Library of Arabic Literature

For more details on individual titles, visit www.libraryofarabicliterature.org

Classical Arabic Literature: A Library of Arabic Literature Anthology
Selected and translated by Geert Jan van Gelder (2012)

A Treasury of Virtues: Sayings, Sermons, and Teachings of ʿAlī, by al-Qāḍī al-Quḍāʿī, with the *One Hundred Proverbs* attributed to al-Jāḥiẓ
Edited and translated by Tahera Qutbuddin (2013)

The Epistle on Legal Theory, by al-Shāfiʿī
Edited and translated by Joseph E. Lowry (2013)

Leg over Leg, by Aḥmad Fāris al-Shidyāq
Edited and translated by Humphrey Davies (4 volumes; 2013–14)

Virtues of the Imām Aḥmad ibn Ḥanbal, by Ibn al-Jawzī
Edited and translated by Michael Cooperson (2 volumes; 2013–15)

The Epistle of Forgiveness, by Abū l-ʿAlāʾ al-Maʿarrī
Edited and translated by Geert Jan van Gelder and Gregor Schoeler (2 volumes; 2013–14)

The Principles of Sufism, by ʿĀʾishah al-Bāʿūniyyah
Edited and translated by Th. Emil Homerin (2014)

The Expeditions: An Early Biography of Muḥammad, by Maʿmar ibn Rāshid
Edited and translated by Sean W. Anthony (2014)

Two Arabic Travel Books

Accounts of China and India, by Abū Zayd al-Sīrāfī

Edited and translated by Tim Mackintosh-Smith (2014)

Mission to the Volga, by Aḥmad ibn Faḍlān

Edited and translated by James Montgomery (2014)

Disagreements of the Jurists: A Manual of Islamic Legal Theory, by al-Qāḍī al-Nuʿmān

Edited and translated by Devin J. Stewart (2015)

Consorts of the Caliphs: Women and the Court of Baghdad, by Ibn al-Sāʿī

Edited by Shawkat M. Toorawa and translated by the Editors of the Library of Arabic Literature (2015)

What ʿĪsā ibn Hishām Told Us, by Muḥammad al-Muwayliḥī

Edited and translated by Roger Allen (2 volumes; 2015)

The Life and Times of Abū Tammām, by Abū Bakr Muḥammad ibn Yaḥyā al-Ṣūlī

Edited and translated by Beatrice Gruendler (2015)

The Sword of Ambition: Bureaucratic Rivalry in Medieval Egypt, by ʿUthmān ibn Ibrāhīm al-Nābulusī

Edited and translated by Luke Yarbrough (2016)

Brains Confounded by the Ode of Abū Shādūf Expounded, by Yūsuf al-Shirbīnī

Edited and translated by Humphrey Davies (2 volumes; 2016)

Light in the Heavens: Sayings of the Prophet Muḥammad, by al-Qāḍī al-Quḍāʿī

Edited and translated by Tahera Qutbuddin (2016)

Risible Rhymes, by Muḥammad ibn Maḥfūẓ al-Sanhūrī

Edited and translated by Humphrey Davies (2016)

A Hundred and One Nights

Edited and translated by Bruce Fudge (2016)

The Excellence of the Arabs, by Ibn Qutaybah
Edited by James E. Montgomery and Peter Webb
Translated by Sarah Bowen Savant and Peter Webb (2017)

Scents and Flavors: A Syrian Cookbook
Edited and translated by Charles Perry (2017)

Arabian Satire: Poetry from 18th-Century Najd, by Ḥmēdān al-Shwēʿir
Edited and translated by Marcel Kurpershoek (2017)

In Darfur: An Account of the Sultanate and Its People, by Muḥammad ibn ʿUmar al-Tūnisī
Edited and translated by Humphrey Davies (2 volumes; 2018)

War Songs, by ʿAntarah ibn Shaddād
Edited by James E. Montgomery
Translated by James E. Montgomery with Richard Sieburth (2018)

Arabian Romantic: Poems on Bedouin Life and Love, by ʿAbdallah ibn Sbayyil
Edited and translated by Marcel Kurpershoek (2018)

Dīwān ʿAntarah ibn Shaddād: A Literary-Historical Study, by James E. Montgomery (2018)

Stories of Piety and Prayer: Deliverance Follows Adversity, by al-Muḥassin ibn ʿAlī al-Tanūkhī
Edited and translated by Julia Bray (2019)

Tajrīd sayf al-himmah li-stikhrāj mā fī dhimmat al-dhimmah: A Scholarly Edition of ʿUthmān ibn Ibrāhīm al-Nābulusī's Text, by Luke Yarbrough (2019)

The Philosopher Responds: An Intellectual Correspondence from the Tenth Century, by Abū Ḥayyān al-Tawḥīdī and Abū ʿAlī Miskawayh
Edited by Bilal Orfali and Maurice A. Pomerantz
Translated by Sophia Vasalou and James E. Montgomery (2 volumes; 2019)

The Discourses: Reflections on History, Sufism, Theology, and Law—Volume One, by al-Ḥasan al-Yūsī
Edited and translated by Justin Stearns (2020)

Impostures, by al-Ḥarīrī
Translated by Michael Cooperson (2020)

Maqāmāt Abī Zayd al-Sarūjī, by al-Ḥarīrī
Edited by Michael Cooperson (2020)

English-only Paperbacks

Leg over Leg, by Aḥmad Fāris al-Shidyāq (2 volumes; 2015)

The Expeditions: An Early Biography of Muḥammad, by Maʿmar ibn Rāshid (2015)

The Epistle on Legal Theory: A Translation of al-Shāfiʿī's Risālah, by al-Shāfiʿī (2015)

The Epistle of Forgiveness, by Abū l-ʿAlāʾ al-Maʿarrī (2016)

The Principles of Sufism, by ʿĀʾishah al-Bāʿūniyyah (2016)

A Treasury of Virtues: Sayings, Sermons, and Teachings of ʿAlī, by al-Qāḍī al-Quḍāʿī with the *One Hundred Proverbs* attributed to al-Jāḥiẓ (2016)

The Life of Ibn Ḥanbal, by Ibn al-Jawzī (2016)

Mission to the Volga, by Ibn Faḍlān (2017)

Accounts of China and India, by Abū Zayd al-Sīrāfī (2017)

A Hundred and One Nights (2017)

Disagreements of the Jurists: A Manual of Islamic Legal Theory, by al-Qāḍī al-Nuʿmān (2017)

What ʿĪsā ibn Hishām Told Us, by Muḥammad al-Muwayliḥī (2018)

War Songs, by ʿAntarah ibn Shaddād (2018)

The Life and Times of Abū Tammām, by Abū Bakr Muḥammad ibn Yaḥyā al-Ṣūlī (2018)

The Sword of Ambition, by ʿUthmān ibn Ibrāhīm al-Nābulusī (2019)

Brains Confounded by the Ode of Abū Shādūf Expounded, by Yūsuf al-Shirbīnī, with *Risible Rhymes* by Muḥammad ibn Maḥfūẓ al-Sanhūrī (2 volumes; 2019)

The Excellence of the Arabs, by Ibn Qutaybah (2019)

Light in the Heavens: Sayings of the Prophet Muḥammad, by al-Qāḍī al-Quḍāʿī (2019)

Scents and Flavors: A Syrian Cookbook (2020)

Arabian Satire: Poetry from 18th-Century Najd, by Ḥmēdān al-Shwēʿir (2020)